DON'T THROW AWAY YOUR STICK
Till You Cross the River

The Journey of an Ordinary Man

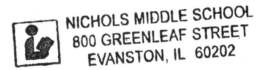

7 20715 50576 7

DON'T THROW AWAY YOUR STICK
Till You Cross the River

The Journey of an Ordinary Man

by Vincent Collin Beach

with Anni Beach

FIVE STAR PUBLICATIONS, INC.

Chandler, AZ

Linda F. Radke, President
Five Star Publications, Inc.
PO Box 6698
Chandler, AZ 85246-6698
480-940-8182
www.DontThrowAwayYourStick.com

Library of Congress Cataloging-in-Publication Data

Beach, Vincent, 1924–
  Don't throw away your stick till you cross the river: the journey of an ordinary man / by Vincent Beach with Anni Beach.
    p. cm.
  ISBN-13: 978-1-58985-057-6
  ISBN-10: 1-58985-057-2
1. Beach, Vincent, 1924–   2. Beach, Vincent, 1924 – Family.   3. Jamaican Americans – Biography.   4. Immigrants – United States – Biography.
5. United States. Air Force – Biography.   6. Jamaica – Biography.   I. Beach, Anni.   II. Title.
  E184.J27B43 2006
  973'.0496972920092 – dc22
  [B]

                              2006037367

ISBN: 978-1-58985-057-6

Printed in the United States of America
Editor: Gary Anderson
Cover Design: Tani Bayer
Interior Layout: Raphael Freeman, Jerusalem Typesetting
Project Manager: Sue DeFabis

My life story is dedicated to the memory of two sons

Jaswan Ali and Lal Ramdin Beach

Contents

Acknowledgments

Without the help and support of many people, my story in book form would not be a reality. I thank Linda F. Radke, President of Five Star Publications, for taking on the project, and for the guidance of Sue DeFabis, her assistant in production, for giving so much support towards the completion of the manuscript, and subsequent marketing.

AC and I spent last summer as guests at a cattle ranch in Shandon, California, in solitude among the rolling hills, with only the cattle and cottontails for company. My brother-in-law Bill Hopper and sister-in-law Janette made that wonderful place available to us – without which it's doubtful I could have pulled my thoughts together.

We asked editor friends Nancy Ross of Paso Robles, California and Judy Hallet of Mesa, Arizona, to read the long manuscript and give us their input and critique of the work in its infancy. They were wonderful in giving of their time. Gary Anderson, professional editor working for Five

Star Publications, contributed his editing knowledge to the book – helping us with all of the technical aspects.

My three children Kris, Sanjay, and Jenny raised questions and delved back into their memories to bring a depth to the story that I might have overlooked. Their insights were vital to my memory and their presence in my life brings huge comfort.

I am grateful to Neil Dela Cruz, a recent immigrant from the Philippines and a member of the Jam Pak Blues 'N' Grass Neighborhood Band, who has given his time in helping with computer know-how and getting the book ready to turn over to the publisher.

I can't forget the chicken soup, warm biscuits, and care that Cathie Lowmiller, our Jam Pak fiddle teacher, brought when I was sick.

John and Judy Hallet of Memory Makers in Mesa, Arizona, have given so much to us in terms of technical support that it's hard to know where to begin to say thank you. From producing DVDs of Jam Pak, to the latest project of scanning and putting captions to the photographs for the book, their help has been priceless, and their friendship wonderful.

I thank Mark and Dianne Hickler who nominated us for Parents of the Year through the Arizona Parent's Council in 2002. That event brought new people into our lives – among them Arizona State Representative Mark Anderson, and gave us encouragement to keep faithful to our neighborhood work.

I'm always grateful for the acceptance and friendship of my sisters-in-law Nyle Hallman, Janette Hopper, and Dr. Miriam LeGare, who have never failed to keep in touch, visit, and make me a part of their families.

Howard and Susan Anderson have been great friends in our lives, including us in their bluegrass music world, giving technical support in music and computers, and promoting the work of the band.

Lyle Barnard has the biggest laugh one could ever imagine and his humor at church and in our bands never fails to lift my spirits and make me laugh, too. That's a gift to all of us.

I'm grateful for Ed and Helen Hamlet of Wisconsin who found us at a bluegrass festival struggling to light a kerosene lamp. Ed lit the lamp, and they continue to be our Jam Pak friends, supplying some "buckets of dollars" when they see a need. They have saved the day several times.

Although our health system in the United States needs a great deal of work, there is one organization which I must thank for saving my life and continuing to provide all that I need – Cigna Health Care of Arizona. They have made it possible for me to visit one of the foremost neurologists, Dr. Johan Samanta, who specializes in movement disorders. His innovative approach to my condition has allowed me the time to complete my life story and hopefully live to have a few more stories. I am also grateful to Dr. Rudolph Cane.

John and Cecelia Tambe-Ebot, immigrants from Cameroon in West Africa, have brought us into their family circle. The approach to family life and peaceful solutions in their homeland village could find application in our society – I hope that they will be encouraged to share their vast experience and knowledge here in our community.

I could go on and on with all the people and family members who bring their gifts to my life, but *that* could take another book. I will end these words of thanks by saying that without my wife and friend Anni, whom I always call AC, there would be no book. She has never gotten tired of hearing my stories over these many years, and indeed, has insisted that they be put into written form. I thank her for everything.

Preface

I'm happy that you've opened the book to this page and I greet you. My life is well into the eighth decade and there are a few stories to tell – of struggle and triumph, of achievement and failure, of love and injury to the human spirit. I'm an ordinary man – I didn't achieve great success by the world's standards, but I achieved moderate success through hard work, perseverance, and through the blessings of Almighty God and Father of the universe.

I believe the stories of other people's lives are enlightening and reveal the fact that we are all part of the human condition. We do not arrive, nor do we leave, in perfection. I used to say, "I eat nails for breakfast" – to mean I was one tough guy, now I sometimes have to be fed my breakfast – but all the years are a great adventure.

A long time ago, for some class, I designed a collage of my life choosing bits and pieces which said, "Vincent did this, he did that, and can do the other." When I finished I was disappointed that I didn't share, "Vincent: these are his dreams, his hopes, his fears, his failures and his frustrations." I hope in this written collage of my life you will feel camaraderie with a fellow human being, perhaps gleaning some thought or idea to enhance your quest for a satisfying life. I also hope that you discover your own application to my mother's adage: *Don't throw away your stick till you cross the river.*

PART ONE
1924–1944

1. Foundation

Although a tiny part of the universe, every baby born is the promise of a new generation. Without fanfare or much fuss, I was born on September 25, 1924. In a small village called Knollis, in the country of Jamaica, the midwife came and helped my mother, Miss Rosa, deliver me. By all accounts I was a healthy baby. My father named me Vincent after St. Vincent de Paul and my mother gave me the middle name of Collin.

Knollis was such a little village that if you blinked you'd miss it. My dad was a tailor making men's suits and collaborated with my mother who was a dressmaker. The steady whirring sound of the two treadle sewing machines with my parents bent over their work are some of my earliest memories. They plied their trade day in and day out while raising my oldest brother Eric, sister Minnette, brother Kenneth and me.

My dad was born in Church Road which is near Bog Walk in the parish of St. Catherine. Grandpa Henry Beach and Grandma Lavina lived close by us. Grandma was a huge, short lady, black in color, and stone-blind who loved to cook. Grandpa was slim, bald, and somewhat red and light in color. In later years, Morocco was mentioned as a country of origin for the Beach side of the family. (Nearly all blacks in Jamaica were there because their ancestors had been snatched from their homes in West Africa and dropped off along the way as the slave ships made their way to North America.)

Grandma would feed us until we could hardly walk; sweet yams, beans, rice, and all kinds of fruit from their trees. Holidays were special: Christmas, Easter, and any other excuse for a family gathering would find us all at Grandpa and Grandma's house stuffing ourselves. The giant mango tree, by the side of their cottage, had roots that rose above the ground which made it easy for a small boy to climb and pick the luscious fruit and suck it from the skin. I loved food so much that my brothers and sister used to tell a story: when I was only a few months old I came rolling out of the bedroom in our little shack in search of food. It's true that I was always hungry, so getting to pick my food became a priority even at a young age.

When I was four, though money was always short, my father signed me up for kindergarten which cost a few pennies a day. We sat on wooden benches outside under the palm trees, singing, and having our lessons. I loved to learn and listen to my young teacher tell stories and read books to us. She told my mother that I was a smart little boy.

My father Theophilus Augustus Beach, called Mas T by everyone including the kids, decided we had outgrown our cozy two-room shack. We moved like thieves in the night with a borrowed truck. Stacked with every last bit of our stuff, we arrived at our brand new wood house with lots of space and rooms. We set up housekeeping at the crossroads of Walks Road and Brunswick Avenue located just outside the city of Spanish Town in the parish of St. Catherine. We looked out at fields of grass and trees and the bluest mountains you can imagine.

Eric, Minnette, and Kenneth had been in a small public school near Knollis, while I was in the private kindergarten. St. Catherine's Catholic School was located about a mile-and-a-half from our new home and my parents enrolled us and paid the fees – money they could ill-afford with such a large family and living off their tailoring business. My mother's efforts at selling her delicious pies and breads at the marketplace helped add to the income.

Our neighbors looked at us and made comments. "You Beaches must be rich. How you make so much money you send your kids to private school?" They thought if you worked at home, you had it made. The comments would fly around and my mother was armed and ready for the fight. *"You get off your big fat ass and work hard you could do the same."* Of all people you better not criticize or question, it was Miss Rosa.

Mother Xavier met us at our new school. A great big nun wearing the traditional habit of the Sisters of Mercy from Boston, Massachusetts, she was the boss. She stood five-feet-two inches with a waistline of perhaps sixty inches. "Vincent, I'll twist your ear if you don't do right!" Over the years I was to hear that voice ringing in my head. Mother came to Spanish Town and lived out her life (she's buried in the nearby cemetery) with a mission to turn us into educated young Catholic men and women. Sister Raymond and Sister Joseph completed the teaching triumvirate at St. Catherine's Catholic School – from which I received all my formal education through the sixth grade.

2. Mas T

My father, Theophilus Augustus Beach, born October 24, 1887, was about five-feet-eight inches and sometimes wore a mustache. He was a black man, not very dark, about my complexion when I'm not sunburned. He wore long trousers, slippers, (which we now call sandals), and a homemade shirt. Bald on top, with silky black and gray hair around the edges, he spoke softly and with authority. No one ever heard him shout. Sometimes you'd wonder if he was there, he was so quiet.

Mas T grew up on Church Road near Bog Walk. He attended a few grades in elementary school. He loved to read the newspaper and every Sunday would find him out under the trees reading the paper to a group of local men. Many guys didn't read well and one of the put downs you'd hear for ignorance was, "You ought to go and get Beach to teach you how to read!"

Mas T would often walk the eight miles to his father's house. There he would gather all the food he could find: yams, potatoes, oranges, grapefruits, mangoes, and ackee, a tropical fruit that tastes like eggs when cooked. He'd sling it all in a sack around his shoulders and trudge home. It had to be a struggle, but we never heard a word of complaint. He felt it was necessary because his children needed the food.

Before my folks were married, Mas T fathered a child named Terrance Beach. Each of my father's brothers did the same thing. Uncle Joseph had a daughter named Rhoda and Uncle Thaddeus had a son named Hezekiah. My grandparents raised them all. Mas T never spoke about Terrance's birth, but he always spoke highly of him and would treat him well when Terrance, who became a master carpenter, came to visit. These children helped Grandpa Henry work the land up in Bog Walk. We never knew their mothers.

Money was always short. A new house, a growing family, and poverty drove my dad to accept a job under one of the foreign work programs offered. He signed up to go to Honduras where he stayed nearly four years, sending home money to take care of us. He had a job as a commissary sales person on a great plantation. He even became a manager as he had a good command of English, reading, writing, and math.

One Christmas, the money my dad sent home each month was stolen from the mailbox. We found the envelope and parts of the letter but we couldn't identify the culprit. The post office was put on alert and it never happened again. But that was a pretty bleak Christmas.

Mas T came home from Honduras when I was about eight. It was a most exciting time as there would be more money, more food and he also brought presents for us. We had no radio in our home, so the best gift was the Victrola Gramophone (a wind-up record player) with four records. We played "Abide With Me" so much that the grooves in the record finally no longer accepted the needle.

My father never left home again. He picked up his tailoring business and also worked seasonal jobs to support his family of five children (Mavis, the last child, was born while he was overseas) in addition to a cousin or two.

I didn't have the privilege of being with my dad when I became a man and a father. But I realize that he had a strong influence on me purely by his example of everyday living. He was pleasant and steadfast and a trusted head of the family. He never raised a hand to any of us. He was always generous with whatever he had and he would never eat and leave the children without. He was respectful of everyone.

Mas T died on June 2, 1953 of what seemed to be stomach problems. It's such a long time ago, yet he is vivid in my memory. Although I never saw him again when I left home in 1944, I'm glad that at least I was able to send him money and clothes that he enjoyed for several years before his death.

3. Miss Rosa

Rosa Rebecca Goldson, born July 16, 1894 in St Mary's Parish, was our mother. Miss Rosa, as we called her, was a sturdy-built woman, about five-feet-six inches and with black, shiny, pressed hair and a medium brown complexion. She was part Maroon which is the tribe of native peoples of Jamaica. She had very little formal education, perhaps going through fourth grade.

I have been unable to find out how my father and mother met or what brought them together. They were so different in disposition and yet I never remember them carrying on a serious argument or showing any disrespectful behavior to one another. There was no open affection although they had one bedroom to themselves. I was to learn later that Miss Rosa and Mas T had eleven children, five of whom were stillborn and a little sister of mine named Sunshine who lived to be about three and died of illness.

My mother could make a joke and go far into being critical with her joke, but woe to the person who tried to enter into the repartee. We might say *that she could dish it out, but not take it.*

Her ways were harsh. I don't remember words of comfort and love, hugs or kisses. "You'll be nothing but a beggar and a jailbird, you no good boy." That was her favorite mantra for me and her belt or switch was always handy. Today, she would be considered an abusive mother and her child-rearing techniques might not be tolerated. Yet, her family was her life. She toiled endlessly to see that we were fed, clothed, sent to private school, and had the best health care she could offer.

Miss Rosa would walk around the yard and surrounding countryside gathering weeds and grasses. She boiled and mixed the awful-tasting potions which we would dutifully drink. For the first two weeks of every summer vacation, we'd wake up to take a cup of Miss Rosa's special tonic to clean out our bowels. One summer the tonic killed forty-two worms being harbored in my body.

This Baptist lady never discussed religion, but she was relied upon by neighbors to help them heal.

"Oh, Mrs. Beach, I have a stomach pain. Can you fix something for it?"

My mother would prepare a weed tonic or give some grasses to the patient to cook and drink. She was the neighborhood doctor and on one very memorable occasion, she was the veterinarian.

Our brown and white cow was struggling to give birth. Now the cow was precious to us and to our mother. Miss Rosa milked the cow using the milk for foods and for us to drink. The calf had turned the wrong way. Miss Rosa went to work. She had us guys lined up as her assistants.

"Get all that aloe you can from the garden. Peel them."

We did that and next we had to put all that slippery stuff in a washtub and begin to squash it all around. When we had a big pot full, she lathered her arms and hands, got the cow to lie down and began to massage the cow's backside and work in the aloe.

She struggled for hours to turn the calf. The cow was ready to give up and die but Miss Rosa, living up to one of her famous sayings, *If it's not dead, don't throw it away*, worked herself to the point of exhaustion. She turned the calf around until it was aimed in the right direction. The cow took heart and began to push again and the calf came. Sadly, the little bull was dead, but the cow got up and began eating and lived for years. The neighbors came and spoke in awe to this sometimes frightening woman, my mother, *"Miss Rosa, you worked a miracle."*

Privacy was of high importance to Miss Rosa – nosy neighbors better beware. Not one to gossip or share gossip, she taught that family business was to remain at home. Some women would sit around with their colorful head-rags and long loose skirts having a field day talking about each other and especially about their own lives. Her private life was never a topic for discussion even with the children; we are left with very little information about her life as a child or that of the Goldson family.

For me, my mother was a rather fearful person and I knew what would happen if I disobeyed or did something wrong. We all feared her walking switch especially when it started to wave. She'd swing it a couple of times and comment facetiously, "Did I miss?" We knew, with certainty, the switch would come down harder and be much more accurate.

Perhaps my mother's methods made me able to function with a fairly high degree of discipline in my life, but some of those early teachings also led to my own lack of sharing thoughts and feelings. I often based my communication on whether a person had a need to know. This guarded approach led to the appearance of aloofness and unfriend-liness. The trait served me well in the military where I received a top security clearance. But in my everyday life I was hindered in my ability to truly communicate. Perhaps this has often been the case of my generation, but, in my later years, I find a great deal of satisfaction and comfort in being able to express myself and let others know who I am.

4. A Typical Day

There we were, the Beach family, in our big wooden house with glass windows, a veranda, bedrooms, a dark-stained wooden floor with homemade washable rugs thrown about, and doors. Eric had his own room, Minnette had her own room, Kenneth and I shared a room, and our mom and dad had their own room. The beds were wooden with homemade mattresses filled with grass.

We all had nicknames which stick to this day. Eric Constantine, born in 1917, was called Con. Minnette, born in 1919, was called Tenty. Kenneth, born in 1921, was called Charley, Vincent, me, born in 1924, was called Son, and Mavis, born in 1930, was called Tup-Tup. We were all growing up in our home in the country and being "poor" was the farthest thing from our minds.

No one had to wake us up. We jumped up at six o'clock on a school morning and jogged the one and a half miles to St. Joseph's Catholic Church hurrying into the pew for morning Mass. The two Sisters and Mother Xavier would be prayerfully waiting for us. After Mass, we'd jog back home and Miss Rosa would have a big pot of oatmeal, or her homemade bread, and a cup of tea waiting for us. She made the tea from grasses and sweetened it with sugar and milk from the coconut.

Back to our two-story schoolhouse we'd go. The school is still in session today and looks the very same as it did in the early 1930s. We'd gather in the courtyard, wearing our homemade clothes; short pants for the boys and skirts for the girls and all of us barefoot. The lines of children would recite the Hail Mary and Our Father and then rush to take our places in classrooms with the Sisters. Slates and chalk in hand, we'd have the lessons of the day.

At the sound of the noon bell, all work would stop and wherever we happened to be we'd recite the Angelus:

"In the name of the Father, Son, and Holy Ghost. The angel of the Lord declared unto Mary and she conceived by the Holy Ghost…Amen. Hail Mary full of grace…"

Then we'd gather in the courtyard under the trees and eat the johnnycakes and fried bananas Miss Rosa had prepared. At times when the dye factory where Mas T worked was closed down due to the season, our mother would say, "You don't have to go to school today. There's no money to get food for your lunch." We'd go anyway. I wasn't about to miss a single day of school. Sometimes Sister would check and then subsidize our lunch. As soon as lunch was over or if there was no lunch, I'd hit the deck playing soccer. This was big fun until it was time to resume studies.

One of my favorite activities took place when Mother Xavier would gather some of us boys around the old pump organ and teach us songs. We'd sing our school song for special events. And we learned my enduring favorites, "Whispering Hope" and "All Through the Night." There were no instruments or other music possibilities outside of singing.

At three o'clock we'd walk home, much slower, no jogging. I'd bring my slate with a piece of chalk and hope that my homework didn't wash away from the rain or humidity by the time I got home. But before any homework could be done, it was time for chores.

Inside the kitchen was a giant clay jar and each kid had to fetch at least three buckets of water from a brook a couple hundred yards away. The rite of passage excusing one from hauling water was graduation from school.

The next thing was to fetch feed for my animals. I had guinea pigs, goats, and a donkey we called Jackass. And we took care of my mother's brown and white cow who was the most gentle soul ever. Behind our house, past some cut-down trees, there used to be a pond and lots of things animals liked to eat grew there. But all that good feed didn't prevent Jackass from bucking me off whenever I tried to ride him. That animal had no tail and a great big temper.

I had my own small garden with a traditional Jamaican fence made of lots of sticks. I planted corn and beans and watermelon and I loved to take care of them. Never did I have to be reminded to work in my garden.

Miss Rosa would be cooking our dinner. In the kitchen, low to the ground, was the stove; a grate sitting on stones with a wood fire underneath. It was big enough to carry two or three pans of food. She would fix red bean stew with rice, a favorite meal for her family, or other bean concoctions. Sometimes after going to Old Harbor and buying fish, she'd cook up ackee (a fruit which when cooked tastes like scrambled eggs) and salt fish. Those two items make up the national dish of Jamaica. She was a super cook and I loved to eat what she fixed. She always made enough to share a dish over the fence with a neighbor or a hungry cousin.

In the kitchen was a table about waist high. The food was dished up on our own plate (mine was white enamel) and set on the table. We'd go get our plate of food and move to the dining room table where we all ate together. When we were finished, we took our plate to the stream that flowed in back of the house. The kids took turns doing the dishes.

Next it was time for doing homework. The kerosene lamp was lit and we'd sit around the same dining table with our slates and chalk, doing our work, and talking about it with each other. If we had trouble our dad or mom would help us. The old man was pretty bright and could help with anything. He sure helped me with math when it came to such things as compound interest. We could borrow books from the teacher to read. But the books were old and tattered just the same as they are today at St. Catherine's.

After our homework was completed, my mother would tell the wildest stories. We'd sit in a bunch and I could feel the hair rise on my head when she was done.

"I want a drink, but I'm not going out in the kitchen alone."

Her stories would scare your pants off, but it was fun. Mas T would listen and make a comment once in awhile.

"That's too far-fetched."

One of the main sources of entertainment back in those days were the street preachers. Pokamia, a group of evangelists, would go to a different spot each night and preach heaven-or-hell and pull in the converts. A lone drummer might sound the call or a trumpet like Gabriel might give a blast or two, and we were on our way to witness some wild religion.

This was our normal weekday routine. Bedtime was eight o'clock and we got into our homemade pajamas and settled down to think and dream about the next day.

5. Mea Culpa

Becoming an altar boy was one of the most important events of my young life. When I was in the fourth grade, St. Joseph's Catholic Church, which was connected to my school, issued the call for altar boys. Today this is a pretty simple, although vital, task. The boy *or* girl learns to hold the Sacramentary (the book in which all of the parts of the Mass are written) for the priest, hand him cloths, and stand by. It wasn't easy in the days when Latin was the universal language of the church service which in Catholic terms is known as the Mass.

Sister Raymond invited Kenneth, my brother, and me to become altar boys. She gave us the Latin passages which we had to memorize. Nearly every day after school, for several months, we gathered in the church to study. When Kenneth and I got home, we used the road in front of the house to set up an altar. There were almost no cars coming by at that time and we could kneel down on the hard surface to chant the Latin prayers and responses while pretending to help the priest.

Although our mother was a Baptist, she helped us accomplish this calling. She would come outside and watch us practice, see that we stayed on task, and also make sure we were scrubbed clean in our galvanized washtub before we helped with Mass.

After much practice, we were ready. We stood up at the altar with the priest, wearing the red surplus and white cassock, and people looked at us with admiration. What a great feeling! To this day, I love the Latin words of the prayers and I can still recite them. That's something I really miss in the new ways of the Roman Catholic Church.

Being an altar boy was the height of my life as a Catholic boy, but going to confession was not. Between ten and fifteen years of age, my biggest hang-up was confession. As I sat in the confessional (the box), Father Owens would have his ear pressed to the screen between us. I would ramble off, as fast as I could, all the evil things I thought I had done. I felt very dejected when Father gave me a stern lecture and some penance to perform. As I grew older, revealing my shortcomings to others became less intimidating perhaps because of my early experiences in the confessional.

I loved being an altar boy and was quite devout in the Catholic faith, even dreaming of becoming a priest, but that didn't keep me from mischief. I liked cigarettes and back in those days one could buy a single cigarette regardless of age.

Another friend named Con, also thirteen years old, and I were chatting and smoking our cigarettes on the road coming home from a church meeting.

Con whispered, "Look out, here comes your dad!"

I replied, "Just cool it. Don't hide and see if he sees it."

Mas T just walked by, didn't look at us, but cleared his throat to let me know he was aware of what was going on. That was his way and he never said a word. If that were Miss

Rosa, she wouldn't have let the indiscretion go. She would have raised hell right then and there, and likely been swinging at me all the way home. That was her way.

Kenneth, or Charley as we called him, and I were often in cahoots since we were the two brothers closest in age. My dad always took his pipe to bed for a final smoke. When he was done, he'd lay his pipe on the floor by the bed. One night after he'd smoked, the pipe was still red hot. Charley sneaked in and took it. Mas T wasn't done smoking and he felt for his pipe.

"Who took the pipe?" we heard him softly say.

We didn't know whether to laugh or cry. Charley hurried back into the dark room and slipped the pipe back where our dad could feel it. Nothing more was said.

Miss Rosa issued an order, "We need extra water today and so you boys get home early and fetch some extra buckets."

After school there was a hot soccer game going and we all stopped to watch for awhile. She only gave the order once and didn't remind us, and like lots of kids, we forgot. So we were just chipping along home and I looked down the road and saw someone dragging along in slippers with her hand behind her. It was Miss Rosa. She came straight up to me and asked, "What happened? I told you boys to be home early to fetch extra water."

And before I had a chance to make up my excuse, she whipped out the big thick belt she had behind her back and smacked me on the head and continued to do so as we ran for home. Charley was also getting his fair share.

I have always hated corporal punishment, abusive language, or coercion for the upbringing of children. I made a vow to never treat my own children in such a harsh manner but rather to follow my father's calm and patient example.

6. Business Ventures

Thrifty habits seemed to come naturally to me. As a boy I had odd jobs here and there. One of the jobs was to help clean out the local water reservoir. I would go down into the reservoir and bring up bucket after bucket of mud. Muddy from head to toe, and aching from the weight of the mud, I earned quite a few pennies.

My dad gave us pocket change which might amount to a few cents. I guarded mine and hid it under the bed. I didn't want my brothers or sisters trying to leech my fortune. After saving for weeks and weeks, I had about three dollars and fifty cents. I asked my mom if I could spend it and she gave permission.

I had my dream of raising an animal and making my fortune grow. I spied an old lady on her way to market with a hamper on either side of her donkey. Peeking out were piglets.

I stopped her and asked, "Are the pigs for sale?"

She replied, "Yes". But she was asking more than I had, so I haggled and got her to accept my offer.

I was in "hog's heaven" being the proud owner of a black baby pig. Lucy was too young to eat on her own so I made a nursing bottle to feed her. This small black pig was full of scabs and bad places on her skin. I washed her with a Lysol solution twice a day. Three weeks later, she had a shiny black coat with a white star on her forehead.

She was the pride of my young life. I had to go find food for her. My mother had let me know that if I was to keep a pig, I had to find the means to feed it. I set out on a campaign to find neighbors without dogs or pigs where I could pick up scraps when they were done eating in the evening. I soon had more food and rotten bananas and fruits than I knew what to do with.

Finding the wood to burn, I cooked all this up on my mother's stove, and my pig grew. I hustled down and joined the newly formed 4-H club in Spanish Town. My chubby Lucy, with rolls under her neck, needed to be bred when she was eighteen months old. She followed me a few blocks to the breeding place which was free of charge for 4-H members.

Lucy got pregnant and I was soon the owner of a huge sow and five black and white piglets. But at ten years of age, I was getting truly burdened. I sold the piglets to neighbors. Then I sold Lucy. My bank account, hidden under the bed, showed major growth. I used some of the money to buy material and my folks made me some new clothes.

I decided investing in livestock was a good way to make money, and my next venture was to buy a goat. Feeding Lucy Two, a healthy brown and white half-grown goat, was much easier than the pig. When I came home from school, I'd take her for a walk and she could feed along the road.

This venture was just as successful as the pig, but it was all getting to be too much for me to handle. Everyone else was playing and I was running around trying to find food for my animals. I also had the worried thoughts of a young kid that there was a war in Europe and they might come for me and what would happen to my animals. After a few months, I sold Lucy Two and bought two chickens. They ended up being Sunday dinner and that was the end of my animal husbandry for the time being.

Actually, that was the end of my business ventures. Not by design, because I had the idea that I might become a chicken farmer after my military career. I toyed with other possible business ideas such as locksmithing. As way led onto way, I never became my own boss.

7. Other Lessons

Constantine Martin, called Con, was a friend of the younger neighborhood boys. He stood short at five-feet-three inches, small shoes, and a huge sense of humor. He could change the sorrowfulness of any situation with stories and wit. Con had no formal education and he served as a houseboy for the Atkins, a prominent plantation family.

Con took it upon himself to be the mentor and tutor in sexual matters to the neighborhood boys. I know that my parents would have objected strongly had they any idea of what he was teaching us.

Con cooked food late at night and he'd invite some of us to come eat. My friends and I would jump the fence and go loaf around his shack to eat and talk. He told us about the girls he'd been with. As none of us had any experience, he'd hold us in awe telling us all the details.

I asked, "When you meet a girl, how are you going to get her to do what you want?"

Con explained, "The next time you meet a girl and you want to do something, you have to come out plainly and say what you want, because the girl might be too shy to let on she's eager, too." And he went on with further instruction.

I was friendly with a girl named Treasha who lived down the road with her mother and sister. I decided it was time to see if Con's information worked. I walked by her house and saw her alone.

I said, "Hey, whatcha doing? Do you have any cold water?"

She brought out a pitcher of lemonade and poured me some. After some preliminary chit chat about sexual possibilities she said, "If we do anything it'll have to be under the bed."

I said, "The bed's too low to get under." I was already getting cold feet over the prospects.

We lay on the floor and she played with the hair on my head and we moved around. She touched me and every time she did, I felt funny. Just in case anyone came, we managed to crawl under the bed. We were kissing but I wasn't sure this was the approach that Con taught us. I started touching her and it was so exciting but I didn't know what to do next. She got disgusted and said. "It's time to go if we're not going to do anything."

I reported back to Con and he informed me, "You can't do anything unless you put it in." He gave me further instructions.

After a couple of other unpromising escapades, I decided to just have fun dating different girls. When I left the island of Jamaica and sailed for England, I still had very little practical experience in the art of love.

8. Work

 I spent three years in the sixth grade because my folks couldn't afford to send me on to public school which cost quite a bit of money. After I'd been at St. Catherine's as long as possible, I worked for a short while as a machinist's helper at Bernard Lodge Sugar Factory. I needed a trade. I didn't want to be a barber like my mother hoped. I chose, instead, to become a mechanic. Following the normal process for learning a trade, I apprenticed at Ramsey's Garage and continued to help out at church.

I had my older brother Eric's example to follow. He trained as a welder but he also continued to serve the priest as an assistant at St. Joseph's. He tended the gardens and drove the priest around. He made sure communion was ready. He had a room at the rectory so that he could assist the priest at a moment's notice. Eric also worked at the sugar factory. He was a welder which was an important job back then. Welder, mechanic, machinist; those were status occupations for the ordinary folks.

My sister, Minnette, became pregnant in 1940. Cambridge accepted the fact he was to be a father, but there was no marriage. Miss Rosa hit the roof. She whipped Minnette unmercifully while we all watched. She tried to chase her out of the house but Mas T, our father, took a stand.

"That isn't going to happen in this house. She's to stay and have her baby and we'll take care of her."

It seemed like one of the few times we had seen him stand up in public to Miss Rosa. In his own quiet, firm way, he saved the day for my sister.

Although things like pregnancy and birth were kept hush-hush, I was there. The midwife came and the baby girl was born. Her first name was Gloria, but I got to give her the middle name of Elisabeth. I liked the fact that her initials would stand for General Electric Company where her father Cambridge worked as an electrician. Gloria grew up in our home for many years and adored Mas T as her sweet and gentle grandfather.

Jamaica was part of the British Commonwealth and did not become an independent country until 1962. During the early 1940s, the Jamaican and British military forces were both recruiting volunteers to serve in World War II. Most of our Jamaican boys wanted to be in the military so there was a big competition between the Royal Air Force and the Jamaican Military.

One day in 1941, Eric told my mother he was going to join the REME (Royal Electrical Mechanical Engineers). Miss Rosa gave a silent consent and off Eric went to Kingston, got a uniform and basic training. We watched him go but there was no joy because we understood people were being killed in World War II.

Eric was gone for a year to Italy, France, and Northern Africa. He wrote and told us how the war was going. His assignment was to detonate land mines. When he found out what his "engineering" job was, it was too late to back out. But he was making money and sending some home for Miss Rosa.

Kenneth was a machinist in the sugar factory. Being a born hustler, he always had a smile and a plan. Although he had lots of girlfriends, Gwendolyn, a gorgeous girl, and he decided to get married. They planned their wedding but a big controversy arose. He could make more money to send home by going into the military.

Kenneth said, "Hell no! I want no part of it."

The wedding didn't take place, but he and Gwen continued their relationship and opened a small shop with Gwendolyn as a dressmaker. Kenneth remained at the sugar factory. They lived together and were making a go at life.

My little sister Mavis was still a student in school and continued to follow the routine of the Beach family until she graduated from St. Catherine's.

9. The Death of Mother

A hush had fallen over our cozy and busy home. I couldn't tell when it began, but as we kids nosed around and tried to listen in, we realized that my mother had a severe stomach illness. To this day, we don't know what it was. We took her to the doctor in Spanish Town and he gave her a big jug of medicine. That didn't work.

We got transportation and took her to a doctor in Linstead that was supposed to know his stuff. She had pains and cramps and I think now it might have been cancer, but no one knew about cancer in Jamaica at that time. All we knew was that she was very sick, and we tried to be quiet.

On a Thursday, about two o'clock in the afternoon, my sister Minnette fixed our mother some lunch. Miss Rosa said she didn't feel good. And right then and there, while Minnette held her head in her lap, Miss Rosa died. The date was February 4, 1942 and my mother was only forty-seven years old.

I was coming home from work and Mavis from school.

We saw someone building a watch shed in the yard. In Jamaica, when somebody dies, there isn't room in the house for all the people who come to visit and sing. So the watch shed is built of posts and coconut branches. We knew what it was, but we didn't bust out crying. Minnette told us what had happened. Mas T was in the yard trying to help get the shed built.

We went into the bedroom to see our mother. I didn't say anything out loud. But inside I said a little prayer. "Thank you, Lord, for her pain is over."

One of the first things I did after I acknowledged her body, was to run to the church to tell Father Owens. We would be ready by Friday and we needed him to come and have the Catholic service and burial. My dad gathered up men to dig the grave behind the house. Minnette did a super job of getting things prepared.

We had good carpenters in our midst. Joseph Beach, our cousin, my brother Terrance, who was a master carpenter, with a helper built the wooden box for my mother's body. They varnished the outside to make it shiny.

On Thursday night the people came by the droves. We were giving out rum and beer to the singers who would sing hymns all night in the watch shed.

By Friday afternoon everyone had gathered, the coffin was finished, and all the preparations were in order. Father Owens arrived and said the Mass for the Dead even though my mother was a Baptist. The pallbearers, who were my brother and cousins, all bigger than me, carried the coffin to the grave behind our house. At the close of the ceremony they put the casket in the hole. No flowers were thrown in the grave, although a box of matches, falling out of someone's pocket, landed on the coffin and weren't retrieved.

There was no outward emotion from me or most of the

people. My father was just himself, taking care of everything. An open invitation was issued to anyone who wanted to sing through that night and the next. Some of the more true believers went back in the watch shed to stay and sing. There was a feast with all the food prepared by my sister and friends and relatives. And the rum and beer continued to be served.

The watch shed was left in place for the requisite nine days and on the ninth day the singers came and sang again. Then the shed was pulled down and we went on with our lives – without the powerhouse of a mother who kept everything, and everyone, whipped into shape.

10. Goodbye, Jamaica

After Miss Rosa died, my older sister Minnette became the mother of the household and raised Mavis, as well as her own child Gloria. There was some insurance money and she managed the family finances and kept the household together. She became an accomplished dressmaker, rented half a store near the marketplace in Spanish Town, and established a successful business.

My dad was working at the dye factory where indigo dye was made from indigo plants. He continued to do his tailoring business, and indeed, any work available to provide income for the family. We talked over our plans and hopes and dreams with him and the fact that there was little future in Jamaica. With World War II becoming more intense, there was increased interest in the military as a way out of poverty.

I was still serving as an apprentice mechanic at Ramsey's Garage. I learned to work on old cars from the twenties and thirties that were always in need of repair. That experience has come in handy over the many years of working on my old cars as well as those of my sons. There were other odd jobs, but I was not advancing in life.

I received a letter from my older brother Eric with details of his military life in World War II. I became more interested in military service and soon received a letter from the Jamaican Military Establishment with a headline that read, *To Mr. Vincent Beach.* It was an invitation to join and a request that I appear for the usual tests. On recruiting day each military service was represented including the Army, Navy, Royal Air Force, and the Jamaican Military. I told the officials I wanted to join the Royal Air Force.

I took the tests and, two weeks later, the reply came which stated, *Welcome to the Royal Air Force.*

Soon after, I was standing in line, getting a number for induction (715546), and getting sworn in. I got to the camp in Kingston and started drilling. We wore our street clothes which were falling apart by the minute. During this time of preliminary training, the guys would gather in the evenings in our camp and discuss: *Is this the best thing to do? You know there's a war out there and they kill people.*

One might ask the question, "Why was Britain coming to Jamaica to get soldiers to fight a war in Europe?" Jamaica was a colony of Great Britain, its independence not achieved until August 6, 1962. Badly in need of forces to fight the war on many fronts in Europe, Jamaicans, as colonials, were recruited and made to feel welcome in the British forces.

We drilled and drilled and drilled. In four weeks time we learned to march and salute. The big day arrived when we were given our military uniforms and we marched around downtown Kingston showing off our fancy footwork. I went back home on three days leave to see my dad and family. *Whatcha doin' in a uniform and in the war?* people quizzed. Leaving the homeland to fight, what was perceived to be a strictly foreign war, was viewed by some as preposterous and very dangerous.

I spent two nights with the family and then it was time to return to Kingston. While I was waiting at the train station located just behind our house, I looked back. My dad was coming. He greeted me nicely and said, "I'm glad I caught you here because I missed you at the house to tell you goodbye."

We talked about things like the house, the yard and the war.

He said, "I hate to see you go, but I know there is nothing here for you." With that, and a final admonition, "Be careful, Son", I boarded the train and that was the last time I saw Mas T.

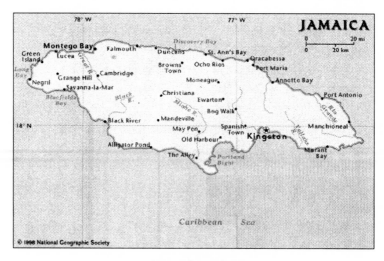

Map of Jamaica

Mas T

Miss Rosa

Grandpa and Grandma's home on Church Road near Bog Walk

*My sister, Minnette, on her
wedding day in the dress
she designed and made.*

My brother, Kenneth

Mother Xavier of St. Catherine's Catholic School.

Praying "The Angelus" in
the courtyard just as we
did in the 1920s and 30s.

Monica, a neighbor, helped
prepare a feast like Miss Rosa
once did in our backyard.

Just like my goat, Lucy Two.

My mother's grave behind our house.

The train, though much more modern, still runs behind our home. This is the place where I bid Mas T farewell.

Children work hard in Jamaica.

44

PART TWO
1944–1956

11. The SS Cuba

I felt lost and somewhat afraid as I boarded the train for the short ride to Kingston. We got to the military assembly and were told that we'd move out in a couple of days. On Sunday there was a lock-down. No passes were issued and we couldn't talk about the war. The officers were afraid we'd take off and run back home. They had us in sections: Group One, Group Two, and Group Three. We got our marching orders and were told we'd soon be getting on a ship.

Men started crying. We couldn't have visitors. Girls lined up along the barbed wire fence surrounding the camp and were calling out, "Let's get married." The military provided an allotment that could be sent home to wives. Preachers were moving along the fence performing some last minute weddings with the bride and groom on opposite sides of the wire.

The camp commander finally seemed to take pity and let legitimate wives and girlfriends in for a visit. I had no one to visit me. The days dragged on while we marched and drilled and finally were told to pack our big duffel bag with everything. Trucks lined up and the crying began again.

Finally, we were on our way to the pier and saw the SS Cuba which would carry us to England. "Would this old tub make it?" we wondered. Soon, we were marching in single file along the pier and the crying and sobbing continued especially among the older men. It seemed like this was a funeral procession. We knew that we were going into a very dangerous war with bombing and blitzing. I didn't think about crying as I was young and looking forward to something new.

We felt the ship moving. Tears flowed again. Some of the men were frightened not only of the prospects of war, but of leaving home for the first time. No one would tell us what was going to happen. There were grumblings: "We're not important; just fodder for the war." The tugs came and pulled the ship out to the main channel and soon we were in the Caribbean Sea.

The ship picked up its own power and we sailed towards Cuba, only to pass by. All I could think as I looked out upon the vast ocean was, *How small we are!* It was an exciting thing for me who had never been anywhere. They passed out sea rations that resembled dog biscuits and orange juice.

On a Sunday morning, we docked in New York City. I could see all the great tall buildings and the Statue of Liberty. What a sight! I'd never seen anything so majestic. It was the third day and we were all confined to the ship. If they had let us off, I know some of the guys would have been on their way to Kentucky in a jiffy.

We picked up other men going to war. On Monday the ship blew its horn, making a huge and shaking sound, and we were soon sailing up the St. Lawrence River. Nobody would tell us what we were doing or where we were going. We went all the way up to Canada, sailed along the Canadian border for a time, and then opened out onto the great mother Atlantic Ocean. When we awoke from a night's sleep, there was no more land in sight.

We were in this ship the crew referred to as a "Stink Bucket" because it was. Around the eighth day, a lot of prayers were being said silently and aloud. Everyone was scared the ship wouldn't make it. It seemed like such a tiny vessel in the middle of the vast and endless ocean

I was scared. One night we felt the ship bounding around like a little toy in a big pot of juice. Big waves were hitting the sides. A terrific storm had hit us. And, from the experienced sailors, we started hearing stories about big ships going down in just such storms.

I was sleeping when the ship blew its emergency whistle over and over on another scary night. "Not now!" I thought, "I'm just getting started." The SS Cuba was firing off torpedoes because a German submarine had been spotted. The depth charges exploded, after they hit the water, causing the entire ship to shake like a car hitting the worst possible speed bump.

Most of the older men were in my group and two of them were preachers. We were already twenty-three days on the sea and everyone was frightened. Preacher Joe Bell wanted everyone to join in prayer, thinking our ship was lost. He prayed, "Lord, help our ship to find its way and we pray to be spared from the peril of the sea. This, we ask, through Christ our Lord, Amen." Our voices lifted as we sang "Nearer My God to Thee".

The SS Cuba sailed another day or so and land was sighted. We weren't lost after all. Eight days later, we were sitting in Glasgow, Scotland. We got off the ship and threw our bags in the back of trucks lined up to receive us. We were transferred to a train where Red Cross workers brought us treats, medicines, and a big welcome.

The train filled and we traveled to a place called Filie in Yorkshire, England. It was a seaport resort closed for the winter which the RAF had taken over for a basic military training camp. The second part of my adventure, after leaving my homeland, was about to begin. I only remember feeling a huge sense of relief that I hadn't drowned at sea.

12. Royal Air Force

We arrived at the training base, à la summer resort, later that evening. We lined up to get our bedding which consisted of seven gray wool blankets. I had never been so cold in my whole life. Our quarters were called chalets heated only by one small pipe running from room to room.

I tried to make some friends and do the best I could. Everyone was resigned to do the same. The date was November 22, 1944, and I was just plain frozen.

We had blankets and uniforms. We were shown how to make a military bed with blankets only. On Monday, the first day of training, we were taught how to put up our pup tents. We would have to camp out two nights with a pup buddy. And we ran everywhere saying, "Yes, Sir, Yes Sir!" to generate a little heat for our warm Jamaican blood.

After the first week, I was getting used to boot camp. Best of all was the super food. We got all the potatoes we wanted, lamb stew, and although eggs were rationed, we each got one egg for breakfast. We usually had oatmeal porridge and the cook gave us a little extra sugar, which was also rationed, as we were from "sugar land".

The military brought Laurie Constantine, a world famous cricketer from Jamaica, to perk up the troops. Laurie, who played for Australia, England, and Jamaica, went from camp to camp where there were soldiers from the Caribbean to try and keep us from feeling too bad and homesick. The military establishment, even in the midst of war, was doing all it could to make the Jamaican guys feel better and at home.

The training was really tough and, into the seventh week, we were crawling on the ground under barbed wire while other airmen were firing over our heads. This was all necessary for future reference. The Germans were blowing everyone away. The war came to us, not us to the war.

The Germans had pilot-less bombers called v1s and v2s. The bombers would fly over Hull about twenty-five miles from our station and it was deadly serious. We would hear the sirens and dash for the underground shelters until the all-clear signal sounded. Once in awhile, we were out of electricity for a few days after the bombs hit a power station.

Finally after eight weeks, I was a full-fledged trained airman in the Royal Air Force. There was a big celebration with a good dinner and lots of special treatment.

Following completion of basic training, I was reassigned to Midland as a Works Hand. My job was to help secure the air base. I was soon sent to Blackpool, a resort town in England, for eight weeks of mechanic training. After my mechanic training, I was assigned to Gloucester, located south of London, for my permanent station. I learned to drive the troop bus and settled in for the duration of the war.

13. First Time

Women were not on my mind until the end of basic training. The fellows had been talking, in fact most of the time, about their various accomplishments with the ladies. To date, I hadn't experienced anything like what they were talking about.

After work we'd go to the local pub each night to play darts, dance, and drink beer. As I didn't drink much, I usually had a soda pop and sat and watched. One night, a girl named Kathleen came up and asked, "What are you doing?"

"I'm standing here," I replied.

"Let's go outside," she implored.

I went outside with her and she kissed me and my body seemed to go crazy. After all of the years of thinking and waiting for this moment, I was still unsure what I should be doing. We walked to the back of a nearby house and talked. "You want to come with me?" Kathleen asked.

I questioned as to where we might go. I honestly couldn't get away as she had me in her arms. She directed me to a grassy knoll. The whole situation started moving much too fast for me, and I was trying to apply some brakes by saying, "Don't you want to get something to lie on?"

She just sat down and unfolded herself. I didn't have time to ask any more questions. The whole adventure lasted about five minutes. I thought, "Is this it?" The moment was somewhat further dampened when I got up and found a big piece of dog poop stuck to my jacket. It stunk to high heaven. But in spite of that, I felt pretty good that I had entered into the ranks of men who have a clue concerning women. When I got back to quarters the fellows asked, "Did you get anything from that girl?"

"What girl?" I answered.

I went back to the pub the next night and found Kathleen. I decided to pass myself off as her boyfriend. We danced and she announced, "I love you."

"What? This soon?" was my reply.

We had a regular relationship and she was nice enough, but I wasn't in love. As exciting as it was to be with her, I knew she wasn't the girl for me. We had one last encounter and I left her by the railroad station and said, "I'll be back in a couple of days."

I went to London to visit my big brother Eric. I needed time to think and mull over the new experience. I was truly wishing that I could talk with my old mentor Con Martin now that I had been initiated into the mysteries of women. I did not casually discuss such topics with the guys and, as usual, I remained a very private person.

14. Music

Life was tough in Gloucester. I had no wife and I didn't know if I wanted one. I did end up with a nice girlfriend named Dorothy. Her dad was a local cop. In the evenings, after work, I'd take her to the movies and sometimes we'd go the dance hall. We kept our relationship above the covers and so I had less worry.

My job during this time was working as an automobile mechanic on military vehicles. I moved up to a supervisory position and my job was to inspect vehicles coming back from the war front. We'd put a classification on them such as "serviceable" or "ready for the dump". There was lots of paperwork and I did that job for about three years.

June 8, 1945 – Unconditional Surrender – VE Day! With the celebration of Victory in Europe, there was great jubilation. I was alive and well and the war was over. My time came for separation from the RAF and I was questioned: "Would you like to stay in the RAF or go back to Jamaica?" I was so grateful to have a choice because such an opportunity was rarely offered to the men from home. My worth must have been felt, and I made the choice to stay in the RAF. That was a crucial decision and my answer changed the course of my entire life.

The RAF graciously accepted me as a re-enlistee. I took my oath and signed papers in October 1946 and was promoted to the rank of LAC – Leading Air Craftsman. A bonus of quite a few pounds went with re-enlistment. The money was of great importance to me; one of the first things I bought was a clarinet I'd seen in the pawn shop. I was listening to Benny Goodman and Artie Shaw and I wanted to become a clarinet player. I had no knowledge at all of the clarinet or of music, and I tried to teach myself to play. That's a hard way to go for one who is just a rookie. After a couple of years of struggling on my own, I finally found a teacher and took lessons once a month.

After I got my bonus, I still had to serve out three more years. I was living in the barracks and trying to play my clarinet in my spare time.

I met up with my brother Eric every two or three weeks in London. When the war was over, he took his discharge from the army and became a civilian, making his life right there in London. Eric never returned to Jamaica until I took him forty-five years later.

I continued as a mechanic and supervisor, servicing military vehicles of all kinds. I had a lot of night duty during those three additional years. I played cards and in-house games with the guys when the work was done. I listened to the radio in any spare moment trying to copy the music of the greats. I was also able to study clarinet at Wrexham Technical College in North Wales.

In October 1949, my re-enlistment time came up and I chose to get out. I felt bad because the RAF had a lot to offer and had given me the opportunity to reach up. However, music was all I could think about and I knew I had to pursue it full-time. I was in my mid-twenties with the thought of making a career in music for which I had no background or training. I thought to myself, "*Lord, this is my supreme challenge.*"

15. Practice Somewhere Else

I rented a room in the house in Victoria where Eric lived with Janet. Both Eric and I studied the clarinet, took lessons every Saturday morning, and we started to get better.

I practiced and practiced until the landlord said, "No more in my house. Practice somewhere else!" I sure didn't expect that, so I kept right on and he called the police. They told me that the landlord was within his rights to request that I not practice in the house.

I joined some other musicians and rented a studio where we could play on Saturdays. That was sickening. I lived somewhere and couldn't practice. I thought, "Now, I'm stuck with music and I can hardly play." I needed every minute I could find to improve on my clarinet.

Eric, and a guy named Barris Reed, came up with the idea to buy a house near Cricklewood. I loaned Eric his share of the down-payment. The house had six rooms and a kitchen. I was expecting to get one room but, as it worked out, there was no room for me. Barris and Eric each took three rooms. For several days I stayed at the Salvation Army and sometimes with friends. A couple of weeks later, Eric felt bad and invited me to come and stay.

Eric had married Janet in May of 1948: I remember that date because, when I visited them in 1998, I helped to celebrate their fiftieth anniversary. She already had Raymond, a cute little two-year-old, and Kevan was on the way. I attended their wedding. Janet was a beautiful woman with a great shape. Eric's buddies and me, all in our suits and hats, went down to the courthouse to witness the marriage. My fairly carefree days were over as living in Eric *and* Janet's house was a new story.

I stayed at the house with them for awhile after they were married, although I felt like an intruder. I mostly ate out but sometimes Janet fixed something for me. All I did was practice my clarinet. Other guys came to the house and also practiced. It was great to blow our horns without someone pounding on the wall. Eric was working as a welder in an automobile factory and slowly, but surely, his married life was removing him from music.

I slept on the couch, but at least I could do what I wanted. I got the idea that if Eric could buy a house, so could I. I located Number One Blundell Street in Islington and looked around to find someone to put up half of the down payment. I ran into an old buddy named Leonard who was a boxer, also from the Caribbean, and on someone's couch like me.

We put together a down-payment and bought the house; six rooms on three floors. My investment looked like it would pay off. The gas and electricity were metered so no one could cheat us. We were able to meet the monthly mortgage. We each had three rooms. I lived in one room and rented the other two. We bought used furnishings from the vendor down the street, so we had furnished rooms for rent. I could practice whenever I wanted, even in the middle of the night.

By this time I found a clarinet player, Charles Jacob, who also taught and I studied with him and also continued to take formal lessons. I made enough from rent to pay the monthly mortgage with some left over for food. There was a rice shortage in England because too many Jamaicans had come on the scene. We broke spaghetti up in small pieces to make pretend-rice and added fish which was plentiful and cheap in London. Red beans rounded out our daily menu.

After working on the music for a year at Blundell Street, we were set to jam. By this time, I'd found lots of budding musicians ready to get into music and my room was headquarters for the band to come. Peter Truman, a saxophone teacher in London, (I already had bought my old tenor sax, the one I still play), gave me one lesson a month. During this time, Eric was still on the clarinet, but Janet was pretty sour about the music. She didn't want Eric to put time into it and she put up all she could to kill it. Even though Eric had his own house, he couldn't blow his horn. He was making good progress, but he had to come to the Blundell Street house to practice.

Joe Harriett, a guy in London who also came from Jamaica, was a good saxophone player. He helped us learn to play and every Sunday we'd have a jam session at our place with four or five guys. Each jam member would call a tune and then teach the others how to play it. Men like Joe were the ones who pushed us ahead and taught us how to be a band.

I was living off my bank account which had accumulated from the Royal Air Force. I looked for a job, although I wasn't in too big a hurry to find one. But I couldn't forget my family whom I left in Jamaica in 1944. The family at home always appreciated the money I sent to help them. I received a nice letter from my older sister Minnette, written May 20, 1949, with a picture of her little girl Gloria (Miss Plum). She stated, "I thank you for that which you have sent me, for out here is very hard." She ended her letter asking for photos and said, "May God bless and keep you my dear brother, my little brother, till we see each other again. Ever same, your sister, Tenty." Whatever I had, I continued to send some money home for our father, Mas T, and the family.

16. Stowaway

My older brother Eric received a letter from our brother Kenneth and gave it to me to read. Written from Jamaica, and dated September 19, 1948, the letter said:

"*Hoping all is well and congratulations on the lucky bride. It seems as she struck a mine, or is it you who struck it. I am waiting to hear of Son's (me) coming off next. As for me, I can only bear that in mind, for the kind of life, I just don't see it as yet. But, boy, when Tenty* (our big sister Minnette) *showed me the snap, I feel great the affection to the unknown bride and was sure warm, but anyway there is a distant ocean in the middle of us. I sincerely hope we'll be seeing each other sometime to give her the happiness of my heart between the two of you. But may the mercy and love of the Divine God be with you two always. And please let me have a photo of her. I besending one of me girl Gwendolyn for you two.*"

Kenneth went on to say, "*Next, I always appeal to you about coming over. I just know you are properly naturalized by now and can help me across. Listen, Brother, I am depending on you and mention it. I don't want to wait until my ambition leaves me. So I'll be waiting to hear from you soon. And tell Son to write. I want to have a chat with him."*

Out of nowhere, Kenneth, our brother, arrived on the scene. He was a stowaway on a ship from Jamaica, sailing across the Atlantic without a nickel. When I left Jamaica, Gwendolyn and Kenneth were doing well, but Kenneth said they sold most of their things and he cooked up a plan to get to England without Eric's help. He had some buddies on a ship and they hid him for the fifteen day voyage, sneaking him food and water.

Kenneth was a small guy, five-feet-six-inches tall, and sharp as a twig. He was always smiling and had an answer to every problem. He was slick! I answered a knock at the door on Blundell Street. Imagine how I felt, after leaving Jamaica six or so years before, to see him standing there with nothing but a paper sack and a big smile.

"What happened?" I asked.

"Nothing," was his reply.

His shoes were torn up and he'd gotten in trouble for stowing away but he conned the police with some story. And in true Kenneth-fashion, he moved to a new city and got one of the better jobs in England; making watches and clocks in a factory that still stands. He flourished. Gwendolyn arrived later, but the relationship was ended when he discovered her trying to attract rich men in a fancy hotel lobby.

We never had a drummer for our Sunday jam sessions and Kenneth never aspired to blow anything. One day he stated, "Hey, Son (my family nickname), why don't you get a drum and I'll work and learn it."

I went down to the music store and told them, "I want to credit a drum set that'll play." I knew nothing about drums and didn't want a piece of junk. I ended up getting him a basic, stripped-down set on loan.

The following Sunday we moved to one of the bigger

rooms upstairs. Kenneth liked the drum set. His practice was phenomenal and he loved playing drums. Two years later he was down at the club gigging. A year after that, he was on tour in Germany with a band he joined. Grass never grew under the feet of my big brother.

17. Debut

I was putting most of my efforts into practicing on my old Selma tenor sax. I learned songs like "C Jam Blues," "Laura," – all jazz stuff. We listened to artists like Stan Getz and Charlie Parker on the radio. We found a woman in London named Mrs. Maude Henry who, for a couple of pounds, would transcribe, note for note, a solo from a record. She had many recordings available, or we could bring in our own. Then we'd study the solo and learn to play it.

A talent night was held at a local dance club where a guy could sign up and play. I put down my name. I had practiced "I've Got You Under My Skin" all week. My name was announced, and I was so nervous going up on the stage. With a piano intro and a fifteen-piece band backing me up, I did my solo. Everybody said it was great. I thought, "Oh, oh America. Here I come!" That was my music debut.

Another club in London issued the same invitation, and I did it again. My confidence was building. While I was doing that, my brother Kenneth was really wailing on the drums. My trumpet buddy James was also working hard.

We were making gigs, having our Sunday jams, and learning new songs as fast as we could. That was my life in London around 1951.

18. A Campaign for America

America – I wanted to emigrate. "Yeah. That's the way to go," my music friends encouraged me. I didn't know where to begin. No relatives, no friends, not a single soul did I have to call on in America. Yet, in my heart of hearts, I knew that if I was to crash in on the music scene, that was the place to go and somehow I was going to make it happen.

In 1951, I visited the United States Embassy and asked a lot of questions. To sponsor one's self required a lot of money. At that time, my account was down to three hundred-sixty dollars. I visited the Canadian and Australian Embassies and even considered South Africa. None were pleasing. I had my heart set on the United States and nowhere else would do. My job was to find a United States citizen to sponsor me.

Hardship was the name of the game. Finding a sponsor was much tougher than I had imagined. "Beach, your chances are hopeless," I said to myself. But I got some newspapers, including a black publication, *The Chicago Defender,* at a local news shop, and began a letter writing campaign in answer to ads asking for pen friends. I wrote to five different people and, within a couple of weeks, a lady answered my request for friendship. Soon, people all over the United States were writing to me, but the answer was always the same; "If you want to come to the U.S., I can't help you."

I continued writing my letters. A woman named Willa Thomas, from Indianapolis, wrote to me and I kept up a steady correspondence with her. She loved my lively letters telling all about the hardships of London. I kept up the letter campaign through 1951 and early 1952. All the while, my application for a visa was filed at the U.S. Embassy.

The Chicago Defender had a notice that the Walter-Mc-Carran Act was being considered by the Senate. That act included thirty-three grounds for excluding aliens from the United States. Most crucial for me was the fact that visas would not be granted to people who were from countries other than the origin of their birth. Jamaicans were severely restricted from immigration to the United States so, as a Jamaican national, I would not get a visa under the very liberal British immigration allocations.

In July of 1952, a letter came from the United States Embassy stating that my application for immigration was being considered. I was a bundle of nerves and excitement because, by fall, it was expected that the Walter-McCarran Act would be approved. My aspirations of immigrating to America, legally, would be next to impossible.

On September 1st, I received a package from the U.S. Embassy which stated that my application for a visa was accepted. I was to report to the Embassy for visa processing. First, I took a reading test, and then I was called for a personal interview. I got a physical and, within a few days, I had my cherished visa. I put my half of the house on No.

One Blundell Street up for sale and booked passage on what-ever ship was sailing to the land of the free.

On December 1, 1952, the Walter-McCarran Act went into effect. This cut off most immigration possibilities for people of color from underdeveloped countries. I breathed a huge sigh of relief that I had been blessed, and I knew that I would not waste my opportunity.

19. Indianapolis

On October 30, 1952, I took my footlocker packed with my herringbone overcoat, some well-worn clothes, music, and my sax in its case to Southampton where I was set to sail. I transferred my savings to the Bank of Indiana in Indianapolis. In my search for sponsors, the only one who would help me was Willa Thomas, my pen friend: "If you can get here, I can help you find a place to live." I said my farewells to my two brothers and my music friends.

I was onboard ship during the 1952 election when Dwight Eisenhower won the presidency. Arriving in New York Harbor, a day after the election, I once again encountered the Statue of Liberty. It was a beautiful sight, and I thought of all those who came before me full of hopes and dreams. In the months to come, I was to question the freedom that the majestic lady represented.

I got to Grand Central Station, put all my stuff on the train, and took the longest ride I'd ever had outside of a ship. I got to the station in Indianapolis and was met by Willa Thomas, a Christian lady, and my faithful sponsor. We were both twenty-eight years old. I was introduced to her friends. She helped me get a room, in Mrs. James Bank's attic, for twelve dollars a week which included breakfast.

I was going around meeting lots of people, sitting in with some good musicians, and I was even in the newspaper. I was introduced to The McArthur School of Music and got registered for the winter quarter at the beginning of 1953.

Wow! I took classes in singing, jazz with my sax, music theory, joined the glee club, and even performed in the musical "Bungalia" as a calypso dancer. Best of all, I could practice whenever I wanted. I was learning so much. The glee club of thirty black men performed in churches and for community events. "Swing Low, Sweet Chariot" and "Ezekiel Saw the Wheel" could just raise the hair on your head. The choirs, the jazz band, and the musical atmosphere were pure joy for me.

Miss Ruth McArthur, founder of the school, was not. I didn't have a car and couldn't afford one. Miss McArthur asked me one day, "What do your drive?"

I replied, "Nothing. I don't have a car."

"I have an old '41 Olds in the back, and if you want to use it, feel free," she said. I took her up on the offer and each morning I had to go and crank it up with the handle on the front to get it going. I used the car for a week and then Miss McArthur set out to make me her yard boy. "Vincent, I sure wish you would wash and wax my car. And after that the yard really needs some attention." She thought I had lots of free time.

"Sorry, Miss McArthur, I don't have time to do that." And without another word spoken, I gave the car back and continued riding the bus.

My bank account was nearly gone, and I needed to pay for my room and the school. I took a job working as a shoeshine boy and the boss wanted fifty percent of what I made.

I complained that it wasn't fair, and the boss man reminded me that I was using his equipment and that was the deal. So I quit. I took a job pumping gas.

In those days, stations all had full-service; self-service hadn't yet been invented. For a dollar an hour, I had to pump the gas, check the water and oil, and clean the windows. I was hired to the night shift. The guy before me had been murdered the week before; stabbed multiple times and the blood wasn't even cleaned out of the bathroom when I took the job.

"Hey, Beach, you shouldn't be stayin' out here all night," cautioned a local character who was hanging out.

"Well, stay with me and I'll get you some blood (wine)."

So I'm alive to tell this story; maybe (like the novel *Five People You Meet in Heaven* by Mitch Albom) he's one of the people *I'll* meet in heaven.

20. Mrs. Hunter

"I would like to work as a salesman in the men's department," I requested of the supervisor in a nice downtown department store.

"Sorry, we don't have Negroes out front. You'll be a stockboy in the back and put the prices on merchandise." That only got me a dollar an hour and I even had to dress up in a shirt and tie. The lunchrooms were segregated. All the Negroes ate together in a small back room. *Lynching* was still going on.

One day a pretty, light-skinned girl came to the department store and I somehow managed to meet her. We talked about the conditions for people of color. "It's even worse for me, being light," she stated. Rachel and I struck up an acquaintance and I ended up in the softest job that I could ever find. Her aunt Sophie was the cook for Mrs. Hunter and I became Mrs. Hunter's chauffeur.

Mrs. Gertrude Hunter was a small, quiet older lady, with splotches of white in her hair. She dressed elegantly, was an avid reader, participated in community activities, and was known throughout Indianapolis. Her deceased husband was an architect and had designed many of the fine buildings in downtown Indianapolis. In fact, one of the fancy hotels he designed had cost six million dollars to build.

She gave me a salary of almost two dollars an hour. I had my own room in the basement of her elegant home where I could practice to my heart's content. Sophie fed me. Wearing my black suit and cap, I drove Mrs. Hunter in her Cadillac wherever she wanted to go. I made sure the house was secure at night and looked after things for her. I would run errands such as to get a bottle of aspirin; and there were no tips for the extras. All change was carefully counted to make sure I didn't short her one penny.

During this time I was receiving letters from my sisters giving me the news that our father, Mas T, was seriously ill with a stomach disorder. As in the case of my mother Miss Rosa, the doctors seemed unable to diagnose his problem or to cure him. I sent money and packages of clothes to try and help. But I had no money to spare for a trip back to Jamaica. He died at home on June 2, 1953, at the age of sixty-five and was buried in the backyard beside my mother. I had not seen him since 1944 and it was so distressing to not be there for him. But I had to continue my journey and keep my goals before me.

After twelve-thousand miles, the Cadillac was traded in. "Mrs. Hunter, there's so few miles on this beautiful car," I stated.

"They're going to give me twelve hundred dollars trade-in and I'll get a brand new Lincoln," was Mrs. Hunter's explanation. And so I was driving around in the finest; just like Morgan Freeman in "Driving Miss Daisy."

During this time, I continued my schooling at the conservatory. Mrs. Hunter allowed me to work around my classes. As she always wintered in Miami, Florida, Sophie

and I packed everything and closed down the house in Indianapolis. Mrs. Hunter got us two train tickets and we went
to Florida to get her winter home prepared.

All the beauty imaginable was there, but as a black man
I had to report to the police station and get a pass with my
picture on it. Negroes weren't allowed in Miami Beach after six o'clock at night. I was truly fed up with these indignities and the inherent dangers of being a black man in
America.

I had a chauffeur's room in the fine winter home. I drove
Mrs. Hunter's little Plymouth to the airport and picked her
up a few days after our arrival. I planned to quit the job after I got back to Indianapolis but I didn't want to abandon
my employer for the winter. I drove Mrs. Hunter places including a Miami Chamber of Commerce dinner. She was
a stock market participant and continued to follow up on
her husband's business, keeping abreast, along with her son
and daughters, of various business projects of the Hunter
family.

I wasn't sure what to do, but I was finished with the
conservatory after the spring of 1954. Most of the men in
the music school were returning GIs from Korea and were
paying their tuition with the GI bill. The school had been
doing quite well until it became apparent that a number of
guys were cheating on the GI bill and not attending classes.
The school was no longer authorized for the government
money and began to fold. I could no longer afford the subsequent higher tuition.

While I was in Miami, on a December Sunday morning,
Mrs. Hunter wasn't doing anything and I was wondering if
I should try and go to church. It had been a long, long time
and I didn't know if black people were welcome. I told So-
phie I was going, and I drove Mrs. Hunter's car to Miami
Beach to the Catholic Church. I crept in the back and no

one paid any attention to me. I had been concerned I might get chased out. So I felt pretty good and Mrs. Hunter never spoke to me about taking her car without permission.

Before leaving for Miami, I had approached her and said, "Mrs. Hunter, I'm not getting ahead doing this work; I can't keep being a chauffeur."

She sat me down and talked with me sympathetically. She said, "I never expected a young man like you to wrap up a life-time in a job like this."

"This is only one stop along the way and I'm so grateful for the work that I've been given to do. I will remain for the winter with you and when we return to Indianapolis, I will need to move on. It's a nice job, but my future lies elsewhere." And so my plans were made for a move.

Sophie, the cook and my friend, admonished me saying, "You're doin' wrong, son. This is a good job and you're going to walk off and leave it."

I replied, "I have bigger fish to fry and I've got to see what I can do with music." I had come to America with the hope of getting into a good band and having a secure future. But at my level of playing, that wasn't possible and I needed to review and revise my plans.

21. Land of the Free?

I planned to leave my American dream and return to England. Life in the United States offered more opportunity and more money, but the ways of segregation were more than I could cope with. I couldn't even go to the bathroom when I took Mrs. Hunter to a bathroom. I'd have to run around and try to find one for colored people. There were so many places where I couldn't go. Just when I thought things were improving, segregation, with all its ignorance and meanness, would surface to hurt and humiliate me once more.

An incident happened which flushed over me with foreboding. I won a sweepstake over the radio with the prize being five dance lessons at the Arthur Murray Dance Studio. I went to the studio, introduced myself and said, "Here's my winning ticket."

The manager lady called me into the office to explain: "I can't have white people dancing with Negroes." I was a pretty good jazz dancer and knew what I was doing on the dance floor.

"You didn't say Negroes couldn't enter the contest," I argued.

"That's just understood," was her reply. That statement told me that the public didn't expect me, Vincent Beach, to participate in regular life. I was filled with a sickening feeling and a desperate longing to leave the racial morass behind and return to safety.

So I resolved to return to England where at least I had the freedom racially to do what I wanted. I had already booked a passage, while in Miami Beach, on anything going to England, and paid for the ticket. I had fourteen-hundred dollars in my pocket, and a re-entry permit, just in case England didn't work out.

After returning Mrs. Hunter to Indianapolis, I went around to tell my favorite people, like Willa Thomas, that I was leaving. They all thought I was crazy to be going back to England. I told them all, "It would take a lot of freedom to keep me here, and you guys haven't shown me much." They didn't seem to understand why I was so upset.

I told Mrs. Hunter good-bye and I thanked her for everything. She had shown me the most respect, and given me the best treatment, of any white person I'd met in America. Sophie, Mrs. Hunter's cook and my friend, seemed angry and told me again what a big mistake I was making. She tried explaining to me what I was giving up. All I could do, in reply, was shake my head, and with her final words ringing in my ears, I went to the station and caught a bus to New York City in the spring of 1955.

I arrived three days early for the ship and put all my stuff in a locker and wandered around New York City. I ate hot dogs and tried without success to find some old friends I knew who lived there. I finally boarded the ship twenty-four hours early and settled in on the MS Gorgic, a Greek liner.

Right on the dot, the MS Gorgic drifted out into the sea

and I thought, "Here I go again." Everything I owned was on the ship and I'd bought some presents for the people in England; sweaters and other nice things. We were heading to Plymouth. The time passed by quickly, because I got to sing standards (my sax was packed) with the ship's performers.

The ship landed, I caught a train to London, and called my brother Eric in Cricklewood. I asked him if I could stay at his house for awhile, and if he would help me find a job. He said that he would be glad to help. Eric and Janet gave me a place to stay, but they had the two boys and there was little room for me. At night we'd go out and play. Eric was on bass, having dumped the clarinet long ago. It felt good to be back with the boys.

But Janet started acting unhappy and, in so many words, told me they didn't have room for me. I'd loaned the money to my brother for the down payment on his half of the duplex, which he bought with another fellow. So it seemed she might have welcomed me as they still hadn't repaid the debt.

Janet was never happy with Eric doing music. She didn't think he'd resist the temptations of night life, nor would it add to the family income. But Eric was drinking his booze, playing his bass, and not paying too much attention to the disgruntled state of affairs.

Most of the friends I knew were still there. I played a few gigs, but I had the uneasy sensation that I'd blown it. I was at war with myself for several months. I talked with the old guys and they seemed so shallow. All they worried about was eating, messing around with women, and getting by on their meager incomes.

Kenneth, my other brother, was the only one who seemed to be moving. He had a new set of drums and was really kicking. He'd gotten a little Austin and he was everywhere with his drums. I kept asking myself, "Why'd you come back, Vincent?" Kenneth was asking me the same thing. Although glad to see his younger brother, Son, he was disappointed that I hadn't seen my plan through to its conclusion. He had wanted to emigrate to the United States, but was stopped by all the obstacles which I had managed to overcome. I felt ashamed and very unhappy with my decision.

One smart thing I had done was to secure a re-entry permit before leaving the United States. Three months into my return to London, and after watching Janet and Eric, and the life they were making, I felt I must leave. I told Eric that if they didn't have room for me not to worry, because I was planning to return to New York. I had made a mistake, and I had to rectify it.

Eric's young sons, my nephews Raymond and Kevan, were cute little boys and I enjoyed playing with them and going to the movies. But it was time to go. I bought a ticket to Brooklyn with the money I had saved while working for Mrs. Hunter.

It was good to be back in England, and to see that people could associate without reference to color and race. I had let the racial issues impede the progress of my dream, and so I set out once again to America, with some hope, and a lot more insight.

22. Re-entry

While back in London, I met a former Royal Air Force friend named Caleb. He had been to New York, but had returned to England to a wife and children. He wasn't doing well financially, so like me, he decided to emigrate once more. As he was going to New York, I decided to tag along and try a new place.

I sailed once more to the United States; this time aboard the TSS New York. The time was well-spent – I was given a Certificate of Appreciation for being a Discussion Group Leader on July 17, 1955. I had lots of time to think and wondered if I was making the right move, but I was determined to try again. Caleb and I walked around Brooklyn for a few days, meeting people, and trying to figure out what to do. Eventually, he enrolled in a trade school and we lost touch.

I put my steamer trunks in storage. I had heard of a woman named Aunt Sarah, in Brooklyn, who would put guys up until they got on their feet. I found Aunt Sarah, an elderly person, but she told me she couldn't help me, and had no knowledge of what was going on in the job market.

I rented a room about five blocks away from Aunt Sarah. When I got tired of eating twenty-five cent hot dogs, three times a day, I'd go see Aunt Sarah and she'd fix me something to eat. That was more help than a lot of folks got. I couldn't find a job anywhere. I did a lot of walking around Brooklyn. One afternoon during one of my walks along Bedford-Stuyvesant, I saw a large gathering of people at the corner. I heard a young man declaring *that black people had very little economic power in the American society. Blacks completing university studies were generally in the medical or social studies fields; few ventured into business or into the corporate world.* I listened with rapt attention and heard that the orator was a new leader by the name of Malcolm X. I went back again and again to hear him speak – *black people had to change their way of thinking and moving in the white world.* I was glad to hear someone speak out concerning the sorry conditions that were a plague to humanity.

Needing to change my economic condition immediately, I went walking down the streets of Brooklyn to see if there were any interesting jobs posted. All I saw were ads for hamburger-flipping and other menial labor. Walking further on, I saw a recruiting station right in the middle of Brooklyn. I waved at the guy in the window and thought, "I wonder what it takes to join the Air Force?"

"May I come in?"

The recruiter said, "Sure," and he took me into his office and showed off all the Air Force paraphernalia. "If you want to join, you have to pass the test which is about high school level. If you pass that, then we'll send you over to the hospital for a physical. If you pass that, then we'll have a few security questions and that's all."

That sounded like good news. I told him, "I'll think about it and come back tomorrow." I didn't know if the United States Air Force would be similar to the Royal Air

Force. I also realized that my dreams of being a musician might not be possible for the time being.

I went back and passed the tests. On August 22, 1955, I was inducted and put on hold for a few weeks. I practiced my horn, ate more hot dogs, and waited until I received written notice to be at the Brooklyn Navy Yard.

I asked my friend Caleb to store my clothes and sax, until I knew my final destination. I arrived at the Brooklyn Navy Yard at nine o'clock on the appointed morning. We took an oath administered by a captain and, when it was done, he said, "Welcome to the United States Air Force." I was thrilled.

When a foreigner commits to the military service, the quest for citizenship is much easier and takes less time. I had already secured a document called the First Paper. It simply states that you want to serve in the military, and that you intend to become a citizen at the earliest opportunity.

Once again, I was off to basic training. Like Filie, England in 1944, Samson Air Force Base, in upstate New York, was already freezing cold. I was thirty-two years old and, although I always liked to say that I ate nails for breakfast, the eight weeks of boot camp was hard work. Upon completion, I was to be assigned to a tech school for further training.

Suddenly, I blurted out, "I'd like to be in the band and play my horn."

23. United States Air Force

That was a big surprise to the officer in charge but he said, "Take this letter and go see Captain Gabriel and he'll set up an audition." Captain Gabriel loaned me a sax and gave me some songs to play. Although I was very nervous, I played a cool "Pennies from Heaven." I was assigned to the 3646th United States Air Force Band, at Laughlin Air Force Base, in Del Rio, Texas.

Wearing my basic airman uniform, all I had to do was stick out my thumb and I got a ride back to Brooklyn. I gathered my belongings up from Caleb, stopped to thank Aunt Sarah for her help, and caught the train from Grand Central Station in New York City.

I arrived in Texas and was introduced to my first band. I soon realized that I was at a severe disadvantage, having had no high school band training like everyone else. Guys helped me catch on. But I had to practice hard and learn to march while playing. Practice was no stranger to me, as I was used to a regimen of four or five hours a day. I started to make progress.

The bandleader, a Chief Warrant Officer, was a nice, grandfatherly sort of fellow who appreciated my efforts. Practice and hard work paid off. I was performing in both the concert and the dance band. I especially loved playing for dances at the NCO Club, the Officer's Club, and the Airmen's Club.

I felt great knowing, that because of my perseverance and hard work, I was realizing my dream of making a living playing music. I made a stripe in short order. I didn't fool around like some of the guys. I didn't drink, I never missed rehearsal, and I loved to practice.

The band wasn't very big, so we were all housed in one barracks. I had a white roommate to start with, and when he shipped out, I stayed with someone else. Segregation in the Air Force had died out about ten years earlier. All of the band members ate together, slept in the same rooms, and spent time in each other's company.

I think that was a great thing for the Air Force to pioneer getting rid of segregation. We were all so tired of it. The restrictions and the second class citizenship, even though we were in the military, seemed like the cruelest and most ridiculous idea of all. The cities were still practicing de facto segregation, and Jim Crow laws were in effect in the southern states.

I had some leave, and decided to take a trip to Miami to see if Sophie and Mrs. Hunter were there. I caught a bus from Del Rio and ran smack into segregation; the kind that had made me book a ship and go back to England. There were places I couldn't eat or get a drink at the fountain.

When I got to New Orleans, the relief bus driver got on the bus and looked at me and said, "Hey, boy, you're in the wrong seat, aren't you?"

I said, "No sir, I've been in this seat since Del Rio, Texas."

He went and got a cop, as he didn't care to approach me without support.

The policeman said to me, "The driver says you're in the wrong seat and he wants you to go in the back." So the cop tells me I either have to obey the law of New Orleans or I can go to jail.

"Okay", I said, and sheepishly walked to the back of the bus, full of disgust, and wearing my United States Air Force uniform.

I arrived in Miami and Mrs. Hunter wasn't there. I stayed in a hotel for a couple of days. There seemed to be a fascination and an obsession with race imbedded in the very fabric of American life that I was never able to understand. For my safety, and my psyche as well, I had to learn to live with the reality and try to adjust my actions.

My dress uniform.

Granville March, my boyhood friend and brilliant classmate from St. Catherine's, surprised me in England in 1945 wearing his RAF uniform.

Eric and Janet on their wedding day in 1948 – I took the photo.

Promoting myself as a sax player in London.

My girlfriend, Dorothy.

McARTHUR CHORALIERS: Member of the McArthur Choraliers to appear in a program at the Indiana World War Memorial Auditorium on Friday night. Junior S. ince, first row, left to right, Hershel Duncan, Robert Alford, Willie Johnson, Robert Hill, and Chester Kimbrough; second row, Vincent Beach, Paul Palmer, John Waters, Peter Quebham and George Armstrong; and third row, Randolph Garrett, Curtis Richardson, Zamma Heglar, and Edward Hawkins. Not shown is Lawrence Strickland. Miss Ruth McArthur, Director of the school, will conduct the group.

Clippings from Indianapolis.

Darneil Christmas, a friend from Chicago that I met on a bus trip.

Chauffeur for Mrs. Hunter.

94

The required pass for Negroes in Miami.

Returning to England on the MS Gorgic

PART THREE
1956–1977

24. My Search for a Bride

M y life was looking up and my musical journey was
well underway. However, I was lonely and miserable
without a companion and family. I had put off marriage, or
serious relationships, because I didn't feel I could make the
climb I needed to make with a family. The few young women
that I encountered during those early years in America
were not the ones I wanted for a wife. I felt I'd have a better
chance at finding someone from my homeland who would
be grateful for marriage and glad for an opportunity for a
better life. So once again, as in the quest to find a sponsor
in America, I resorted to a letter-writing campaign.

While at Del Rio, I sent a letter to *The Gleaner*, a Jamaican newspaper, with a request for pen friends. Within a
short time, I received responses from an ethnic rainbow of
twenty-five women. (Jamaica's motto is *Out of Many, One
People* – extolling the fact that a variety of races including
black, white, Chinese, East-Indian and Syrian make up the
population of that island in the Caribbean.) One of the most
intriguing was from Miriam Cooderath. We carried on an

interesting letter exchange and, when she sent her photo, I thought she might be the one. She was twenty-one years old, tall and slim, with long, flowing, jet-black hair, a warm-brown complexion, and exotic eyes. I wrote and told her, "One day, I will come to Jamaica and look at you."

I didn't wait long. In mid-1956, I took ten days leave and flew to Jamaica. Miriam, her sisters, and a brother-in-law met me at the airport. I stayed at her rented apartment in Spanish Town. We went to dances, to the movies, and I spent money showing her a good time. We had a little fun, what Miriam later liked to call "night food," but as she was still a virgin, it didn't go too smoothly. But the feelings were there. She was funny and sweet and put me totally at ease and I was thinking that I could make a life with this lovely, Jamaican-East Indian young woman.

Minnette was also in Spanish Town, so I took Miriam to meet her as I wanted an appraisal from my older sister. She loved Miriam and gave me a glowing report.

We went up to St. Mary's Parish to meet her family. The small house was perched on the side of a hill, overlooking a river. Her father, Ezekiel Cooderath, an immigrant from Calcutta, worked as a farmer. Her mother, Lilian Jackerancingh, although an East Indian, was a native of Jamaica. It was obvious they had a hard life, but they were jovial, humorous, older people, and best of all, they made me welcome.

Miriam had three older sisters and, as the youngest girl, seemed to be everyone's servant. Although she was warm and friendly with me, I could see that she had a very difficult life and that her sisters didn't treat her well. I gave her money to help supplement the small salary she was earning on her job at a store. That made trouble with the sisters, as they wanted some of what she got.

We spent ten joyful days together and, before I left Jamaica, I secured immigration papers for her. She seemed to care for me, and expressed her gratitude that I had come to visit. She was much more beautiful than I had expected – I was truly delighted that my letter-writing campaign had worked this miracle. We both needed each other, and we made a promise that we would marry.

I returned to Del Rio, Texas, somewhat light-hearted, but knowing there would be obstacles to getting a wife out of Jamaica. I got things together as fast as I could and, in a few short months, flew back to Jamaica and we were married at a relative's home on December 29, 1956. Miriam wore a white dress and was fabulous – she filled the bill. I'd been lonely, but now I'd have a wife and hopefully we would grow to love each other.

I never told my own family I was getting married, because I wanted the wedding to be a quiet and private event. In looking back, I know how unfair and rather selfish that was. But, at the time, it seemed that with so many people, and logistics involved, the whole operation would be overwhelming and expensive beyond my means.

Immigration problems had to be addressed – I left my new wife in Jamaica, not knowing when I might see her again.

25. Murphy's Law

I had already moved to Webb Air Force Base as a member of the 3560th Air Force Band, near Big Spring, Texas. I immediately got in contact with immigration, in both Dallas and Washington, D.C., to secure a visa so that my wife could join me. Immigration was not the only problem to tackle regarding my new bride: the priest at the base chapel informed me that I could not receive the Sacrament of Holy Communion because I had not been married in the Catholic Church.

Miriam had moved to Kingston, so I wrote to Father Roy B. Campbell, a Jesuit priest at the Cathedral Rectory in Kingston. He finally wrote back: "There is no difficulty about having your marriage corrected on December 19th, when you arrive in Jamaica. I would suggest that you have the girl come and see me as soon as possible. If she is willing, she can get enough instruction to be baptized before the wedding." Miriam took the instruction and was baptized and I was grateful for her acceptance of the Catholic faith. With approval of my thirty-day leave request, I returned to Jamaica after nearly a *year* of absence and we had one more wedding: Father Campbell, the large and imposing black priest, married us at Holy Trinity Cathedral Rectory in Kingston on December 22, 1957. Two weddings in less than a year, but I still couldn't take my wife to America to live with me.

I spent several days trying to see the United States Ambassador; I couldn't get an audience, but finally met with the United States Consulate and told him that I needed help. That was the third trip to Jamaica in less than two years.

After spending the short time with Miriam, I had to leave again and return to Big Spring. A few months went by and I finally received a letter stating that her visa was approved. I got her an airline ticket, and she arrived in Dallas on a Friday afternoon. Her tears were flowing from both excitement and fear. She had never been farther than a few miles from home, and had never flown on a plane. I picked her up in my Austin and made the three-hundred mile trip home to the one bedroom apartment I had rented in Big Spring.

We set about making a home and getting to know each other. Love began to blossom and she was the companion I had hoped for. I had been on my own for many years and it was a unique experience to have a woman to share in every aspect of daily life.

"Murphy's Law," which states that whatever can go wrong, *will* go wrong, began to unfold. I received orders to the Philippines for an unaccompanied tour. Miriam had only been in the country a short while, and the thought of leaving her alone was almost unthinkable. With no family or close friends anywhere near, I didn't know what to do.

Miriam needed a lot of help in making the adjustment to a new situation. There was so much to learn about living in America and in the Air Force life. That, coupled with being away from her family, put her in a stressful situation. She was young and I was trying to guide her and help her learn everything I could.

I couldn't imagine how I would be able to leave her, but I was afraid to send her back to Jamaica because of possible immigration problems. I mulled over the problem, talked with people, and tried to figure out what to do. I had a band friend named Lu Nonay who was from the Philippines. He said, "My mom's up in Denver. We can go up there and introduce her to your wife and, if they like each other, she can stay there." So we drove up to Denver and met a very kind, older lady; they got along well, and Miriam decided to stay with her. What a break! We drove back to Texas, packed up, and I said good-bye to my Texas buddies. I drove Miriam back to Denver where I left her in a nice, big house with Mrs. Nonay and her elderly husband. We kept in good contact with letters over the following months.

For fifteen months I was stationed at Clark Air Force Base in the Philippines and our bands played for all kinds of special events, visitors, and good-will trips around the islands. But I was so anxious to get back home to my wife.

I returned to Denver and took Miriam to my next assignment in San Antonio, Texas. I was now a member of the famed Air Force Band of the West (539th Air Force Band) headquartered at Lackland Air Force Base, and later at Randolph Air Force Base. Being part of the fifty-member band, led by Major Samuel Kurtz, was a big step for me. The concert attire was dress blues or white-jacket tuxedos. (I still have my tuxedo, and although it has a few holes, I have worn it for special occasions.) I marched in many parades around the state of Texas, playing flute and piccolo, often right *behind* the horses.

Miriam and I found an apartment off base. It was a time of jubilation, of securing our relationship, and my wife was joyful. There seemed to be a serene happiness because we had survived the separation. I did my best to give a lot of time and attention to helping her become acquainted with American life in the Air Force.

26. Two Sons

In early 1960, Miriam didn't feel well and made a visit to the doctor.

We had been married over three years, and the news from the doctor was *great*. We were going to have a baby. We spent the next several months getting baby clothes and other necessities for our new addition. Ultrasounds were not available back in those days, so there was no clue as to the sex of the baby. The pregnancy was without problems, and Miriam was so proud to be carrying a child.

August 1, 1960 was a Sunday. Our first baby boy, Krishna Devi Beach, was born. His head was covered with long, black hair. In fact, he had lots of hair on his body. He seemed perfect in every way, and he was such a joy. Having a little baby to cuddle and play with was a pleasure beyond compare. When he'd do his funny little baby actions, it was more gratifying than I could have imagined. As we didn't have family or friends to help out, we watched him twenty-four hours a day between the two of us.

We stayed two and a half years in San Antonio, and in

1962 orders came to report to Sheppard Air Force Base in Wichita Falls, Texas. We moved with our baby, and made a new home.

A note needs to be made concerning the many moves, especially for a bandsman in the Air Force. A band has a specific number of instruments of each kind. For instance, if a sax player moves or is gone for some reason, another must take that place. In addition to playing music, my technical job was to serve as a clerk for the various bands: typing up orders and keeping track of personnel.

When Kris, as we called him, was one year old, the three of us flew to Jamaica in 1961 to spend the Christmas holidays with our families. Kris was such a cute little boy and everyone wanted to hold him and run their hands through his thick, wavy hair. He always had a smile and loved to run all around and delight his aunts and cousins. My parents were both dead and I felt a sadness that they couldn't see my little boy. I think they would have been pleased. Miriam's parents were still alive and loved meeting their new grandson.

Being the youngest in her family, Miriam had few new clothes as a girl, and it was my delight to have Minnette, my sister, make her several fashionable dresses while we were in Spanish Town. I took home movies of the modeling show as my beautiful wife showed off her slim shape in dress after dress, each unique, and made just for her. She had shoes to match everything. I tried to make up for what she never had and she was happy. We returned to Texas with lots of great memories of the vacation to our homeland.

Finally, after no particular reason for my procrastination, I went to the courthouse in San Antonio with a lot of other folks, answered questions and took an oath. On March 8, 1962, I became a naturalized citizen of the United States of America. It was another milestone accomplished.

The following year, we awaited the arrival of a second

baby. On Thursday afternoon, May 9, 1963, while Miriam was trying to cook, labor began. I was at the base getting ready for the evening Retreat Ceremony that we played each day while the flag was being taken down for the night. I got the call to hurry home, and wasting no time, I jumped in my 1958 brown-and-tan Rambler station wagon.

Miriam's bag was packed. I grabbed Kris and dropped him off at emergency care, which was set up for such occasions, and took her to the hospital. We didn't have a long wait. My job was to hang out in the waiting room, as fathers weren't allowed to be present for the delivery in those days. She gave birth to a second baby boy, and we named him Jaswan Ali Beach. (A salesman from India had come by our home and his name was Jaswan Ali. We copped his name and sent him on his way.)

Jaswan was another perfect baby, and very cute. Kris, being almost three years old, was quite pleased to have a new little brother. There was now a lot more work in caring for two little boys. Miriam's sister Pearl, who had married and emigrated to the United States, came to visit and help with the new baby. That was a successful reunion for the two sisters.

During those years, we attended Mass at the Air Force Base Catholic Church. Each boy was baptized, and we committed ourselves to raising them in the Catholic faith. The name Krishna was considered by our priest to be a pagan name, and he asked that the baby be baptized as Christopher David Beach. We did as he suggested, and it made no difference to me. Jaswan was able to keep his own name for his baptism.

27. Texas

We finished our morning band practice in the concert hall and sauntered back to the practice room to hang out, eat our brown-bag lunches, and watch television. On the black and white screen was the motorcade procession with President John F. Kennedy and the newscasters relaying the information that President Kennedy had been shot. We were glued to our chairs the rest of the afternoon. No more than one-hundred-thirty miles down the road, a drama was taking place that would shake us to the core and, indeed, the entire world. Later in the afternoon we quietly got our instruments ready and went to play for Retreat. At four o'clock in the afternoon, November 23, 1963, the band played "Hail to the Chief" and "The Star Spangled Banner" to a large and silent crowd. Our president who had offered so much hope for the civil rights crisis, and in whom I had taken a personal interest, was dead. Soon the drama left Dallas and moved to Washington, D.C. where the nation mourned and upheaval continued.

New Years 1964 found me still stationed at Sheppard Air Force Base near Wichita Falls, Texas. The bright spot was the conception of another baby. As we lingered in the west Texas sun, we grew more and more wearier with life, Texas-style. According to the calendar it was spring, but in that part of Texas we were already experiencing ninety-plus degree temperatures. The assassination of President John F. Kennedy was very much in our thoughts and the world was still in shock. Everyone in conversation would ask, "How could this happen in America?" Within a few years we would witness more assassinations and the ugliest of activities among those who wanted to keep an entire race of people as second-class citizens. It seemed as if the heart of America was being torn apart.

One might think that following the assassination, the world would wake up, and the civil rights that so many people were struggling to secure would be enacted and enforced. For the black members of the United States Air Force Band, the reality was different. We went to San Angelo, Texas to play for a parade. We were early and three of us black band members went with the other guys to get breakfast and coffee. We were informed that black people weren't served there and we reported that fact to our band leader. He gathered the band together and approached the proprietor and said, "If you can't serve these guys, then no one eats here." That was a big chunk of business – the upstairs of the restaurant was cleared and the entire band marched upstairs and ate. But that was the first time I could remember a band leader standing up for us. When the band went to New Orleans to play for a parade, during another Texas band leader's duty, all the black members had to stay behind at the base because our traveling with the band made *logistics too difficult*. What made that quite laughable was our assignment while remaining behind: we had to paint the rehearsal hall. We thought about painting it *black*!

Daily life had to go on. The new family member's arrival was expected later that year and we surely looked forward to another baby. The big day was planned with much care. The crib, bassinet and clothes left over from the older brothers were all nicely tucked away for the event.

The house was big and old, and seemed to be standing on stilts on the outskirts of town. The people in Wichita Falls didn't take too kindly to black folks living on the "good" side of town, so we took what was available to us. The house, located by a dirt road, sat on a ridge near a big trench that ran like a river whenever it rained. The paint on the house had long since burned off in the relentless Texas sun. The house had the appearance of a gray barn and when it rained the red mud made a distinct contrast.

Years later when I told my sons about the deprivations in west Texas, it wasn't to burden them, but to give an idea of what things were like during the sixties. Although the coming son was tiny in his mother's womb, he may have felt the anxieties we were feeling that spring of 1964.

As we moved into summer there was not a great deal to look forward to except to plant our garden and watch our neighbor plant his and compare growth. He was a strange bird, and we had a lot of fun watching him. The old gray-headed white man had a nine-year-old grandson who lived with him. Our neighbor appeared to be an alcoholic and he apparently didn't want the kid to see him drinking. He hid his bottle by the side of the house and in full view from our kitchen window. We had a lot of fun watching him sneak around the back, take a drink, and get back before the kid got there. It was real comedy.

Tragedy struck a few weeks into the summer. Our

neighbor fell asleep on the railroad tracks that ran close by the house and his body was severed by a train. A relative came and took the little boy and that was the last we saw or heard from them.

It was early summer and I was given orders to go to the Philippines. I jumped for joy! Having been there before, I knew what to expect. It was quite a relief for us to be getting out of Texas. I'm not sure my young guys would have endured the indignities that we had to endure. They were too numerous to recount, but one such experience illustrates the racism that was legally enforced in the state of Texas.

There was a law that no white person could be in a black person's house overnight. My friend George Goodman, who played sax in the band with me, was to leave for New Hampshire the next day. He planned to stay at my house overnight and we were all settled down – the police were called by a neighbor – they came and made George move on. As fate would have it, he spent the night in jail – the penalty for being in a black bar on the black side of town.

28. The Mexican Connection

We tried not to let all the racial mess and strife interfere with our daily activities. Our military orders were ready and we started the arduous chore of packing our things and getting ready to leave Texas. Everyone moved several times in the military service, yet each move seemed to present new problems.

The check-list was long. We would drive the car to the army base, in Oakland, California, for shipment to the Philippines. The household goods would be shipped directly to Clark Air Force Base. But the greatest dilemma was that Miriam and the two boys could not travel with me.

Air Force regulations stated that I had to go first and secure housing before my family was permitted to travel. Miriam was seven months pregnant and the two brothers just four years old and one year old. In mid-July the movers came and got most of our household belongings; we packed up the rest, got into the 1958 Cadillac, and headed west. Though I didn't know exactly how to handle leaving my family by themselves, I decided to take a leisurely trip across Texas, New Mexico, Utah, Nevada and find my way to San Francisco, California. The Golden Gate Bridge was almost as wonderful as the Statue of Liberty in New York. An awesome sight!

My old friend Sebastian, from Jamaica, was a student at the University of California at Oakland. Moving along the California highway with fingers crossed, I hoped that my friend and his wife would be able to help watch after my family for a few weeks. I arrived at the university campus and found them in a dormitory for married couples.

I explained my problem, asking if they could help us find an apartment and watch over the family until I could send for them. With no excuses offered, they turned me down flat. However, they said that we could stay the night and that was the best they could do. We thanked them, and early next morning, we piled into the car.

My scheduled departure from Travis Air Force Base was only six days away and, as I turned the car towards Travis, I was trying to figure out a plan. I checked base housing to see if they would let my family have an apartment in the BOQ (Bachelor Officer Quarters). As I expected, the Air Force would not house them for even a short time.

Near Travis Air Force Base, was a sleepy town called Fairfield, and I hoped I could find an apartment to rent. After driving up and down the dusty streets for a couple of hours, we found a trailer for rent. We were desperate and didn't have time or patience to be picky. A group of Hispanic children was playing by the trailer. I stopped the car and asked the children, "Are your parents here?"

"Yes," they said, and scampered off to call their mother.

A big, motherly woman came outside and met us. She told us the neighbors were all farm workers and that her husband and the owner of the trailer would be back from the fields in an hour.

A few minutes after five, a ruddy little man in denim overalls pulled up beside the trailer and asked what I wanted. "I need to rent your trailer. How much are you asking?"

"It's eighty dollars in advance."

"We'll take it!"

As an afterthought he stated, "There's a twenty dollar damage deposit. If there is no damage, when you move out, you get your twenty back."

"Fair enough," I said. I gave him a hundred-dollar bill and noticed that his eyes popped open. He smiled, shook my hand, and wrote out a receipt on a scrubby little pad he carried in his pocket.

The previous occupants hadn't cleaned the place, but it had a roof and four walls, and we could look no further. We gathered our things and moved in. There was a stove, refrigerator, two beds, and a couple of chairs; all seemed to be leftovers from Noah's Ark. But we were grateful, that by nightfall, we had a place to lay our heads.

29. Worries

We got back in the car and headed for the base commissary to stock up on food and get some bedding. We all felt more cheerful when we sat down to eat our first home-cooked meal since we'd left Texas.

I can't be sure if I slept that night; a thousand things went through my mind. The thought of leaving Miriam, seven months pregnant, and two little boys in the trailer, was frightening. Next day, as the bright California sun came streaming through the dusty window, my thoughts turned to the neighbors. The motherly-looking lady, Maria Gonzales, that we met the night before, was up and about. She greeted us and, in halting English, welcomed us to the neighborhood. She told us that her entire family were fruit pickers, and offered us a basket of fruit.

Over the next couple of days, we struck up a friendship with the Mexican family. Our two boys were having a good time playing with their children. Each evening, family members would bring fruit from the fields, and we, in turn, gave them a few dollars. I asked if they could help watch out for my wife since I had to leave. Maria promised she would do her best to help.

The day came when I had to drive the car to the Army Base in Oakland, and turn it in for shipment. I took a bus back to Fairfield, which seemed a million miles away. Another bus made the trip to Travis Air Force Base, so I took Miriam and the boys on a familiarization-run to the base and back

While at Travis, I told the medical people about our predicament and asked them to keep an eye on her. At that time, I was informed that she had to travel before her eighth month of pregnancy, or she would have to wait until the baby was several weeks old.

The day of departure came fast. Miriam was now seven months and about a week. The baby was due by the end of September or first week of October. I had just three weeks to get myself to the Philippines, find a house, have orders prepared, and set up a flight for her and the boys.

My flight was scheduled for just after midnight. I was in a daze, as I boarded the commercial airliner, questioning myself on all the details I had tried to cover. I was especially concerned about possible emergencies with her or our little sons.

I was jolted out of my restless nap when the stewardess announced, "Fasten your seat belt. We are preparing to land at Hickam Field." It was early morning when we touched down in Hawaii. I had just long enough to pick up some souvenirs, and get back on the plane. The next six hours were spent in worry and concern for those I left behind.

I have told the story of this move, in some detail, to illustrate that military families do not have an easy life. They are often uprooted over and over, have many regulations with which to comply, are separated from friends and family, and in the lower ranks, have a limited income. When I think back on those days, and the hardship of every move to a new location, I shake my head and just say, "Thank you, Lord," that we made it. I also welcome my retirement check each month, knowing I earned every penny.

30. Clark Air Force Base

We touched down and came to a stop at the terminal at Clark Air Force Base. I felt good to be there; if only I could have brought the family with me. As soon as I cleared immigration, I got on a bus and made my way to the dormitory. From there I reported to my new band.

My tour of duty would be interesting in the 600th Air Force Band under the direction of Chief Warrant Officer Leonard B. Burt. It was great that I knew my way around the base. I headed for the Red Cross and laid my story on them and they contacted the Red Cross near Fairfield. *Wow, it worked!* The Red Cross would provide Miriam with a helper, almost like a chaperone. That taken care of, I headed for the housing office.

I was able to get a house assignment in less than three weeks. That was all the time I had; just three weeks, or Miriam would have to wait until several weeks after the baby was born before she would be allowed to travel. I signed up for that house and, before the end of three weeks, hired a man to clean it, and a maid to set up a nursery.

I went to CBPO (Central Base Personnel Office), and urged them to publish the orders that would give my family permission to travel. We were now into September and the orders were mailed to Miriam. With the help of the Red Cross chaperone, on September 15, 1964, Miriam and the boys got on a flight out of Travis.

The flight line told me the plane was on time, and scheduled to arrive at two o'clock in the afternoon on September 17th. I was there with my big, black 1958 Cadillac, picked up my precious passengers, and headed for our newly acquired house. The housemaid and yard boy were standing by to meet my family, and I had to pinch myself to see if I was dreaming.

31. Third Son

Friday, October 9, 1964, Miriam didn't feel well. After lunch the next day, she went into labor and late that afternoon, I took her to the hospital. At six o'clock that evening, October 10th, Lal Ramdin Beach was born – a seven-pound-four-ounce baby boy, our third son. I spent all evening at the hospital, and thought how great it was I didn't have to worry about the children. We had a built-in babysitter, and I was so grateful.

I had already been selected to be the choir director for the base chapel Catholic Church. That Sunday, October 11th, I directed the choir in the old Latin hymns from the St. Gregory Hymnal and we sang especially well. In a few short years, the hymnal would be obsolete, as well as other Mass traditions. Changes were being made in Rome by the Vatican II council, under the direction of Pope Paul VI.

The miracle of another young son made my cup runneth over. I knew that Miriam wanted a daughter; she had voiced that wish many times. But our son was a healthy and vibrant boy, and I heard no regrets or disappointment from

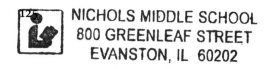

his mom. That was the first day of what was to become a shortened life. There is a truth we should never forget no matter our circumstances: *Life is precious beyond belief and should be cherished, without rancor, each and every beautiful day.*

On Wednesday, October 13th, the doctor said that the baby and his mom would be released to go home. It was a joyous occasion. I brought my 8 mm movie camera and took pictures of mother and baby as they exited the hospital. We drove slowly and talked a lot over the three or four miles to our home.

The house was spanking clean thanks to the superb work of our housemaid. The two little brothers were at the height of anxiety waiting to see and touch the new baby and to ask lots of questions. They wanted to know the baby's name. We called him Lal. It was an unusual name that we borrowed from an Indian gentleman, who was a high government official, with the name of Lal Bahadour Shastri. We liked the name and gave it to our third son. The two big brothers also liked the name, and that made their mom happy.

32. Bandsman in the Philippines

The old adage seems appropriate: *Time flies when you're having fun.* The days seemed to fly by. With our built-in housemaid and yard boy, our house and yard were kept in tip-top shape. The children were always clean and well-fed and cared for. What more could anyone want?

I knew what else I wanted; another stripe. I was an Airman First Class (now known as sergeant) with only three stripes. Although it appeared we were living in the lap of luxury, there wasn't much money with that rank.

By this time, Miriam and I had been married for nine years. Although the military life put extra stress on couples due to the uncertainties of location and moves, separation from families and isolation, I think that we were managing quite well. We enjoyed our boys and we also enjoyed being able to go to the NCO (non-commissioned officer's) Club for dinner as we had someone to look after the children. Our family was thriving and fun to be with.

Christmas, the first with three sons and lots of presents, made for a fine time. We celebrated the arrival of 1965. Lal grew like a weed and, by the time of his first birthday in October, he was taking steps holding on to whatever he could find. I took many pictures and developed them myself in the base hobby shop.

During the summer of 1965, we found out that Miriam was expecting another baby. We made believe that our baby Lal was going to welcome the new little brother or sister, and have a great time. He seemed to understand.

Having the family by my side made my tour of duty in the Philippines bearable. The Vietnam War was in high gear. Our band met the "hospital-ships" each day when the planes, bearing the wounded, would land at Clark. Stretchers were carried off the planes with young men who carried the carnage of war on their bodies. It was a terrible thing to see, yet these brave guys would give the "thumbs up" as we played "Stars and Stripes Forever" and other patriotic tunes. I felt so sorry for these mostly young men. They had been thrust into a situation over which they had little control. We did our best, with the music, to cheer them and let them know we cared.

Our bands served as ambassadors on behalf of America. As part of the People to People program, we traveled to places all around the Philippines. Pigs were killed to feed us in the villages where we were always welcomed with cheers, smiles, and food. The band traveled to Thailand and played at five different bases for the troops that were stationed there.

We visited Formosa, (translated as Beautiful Island, so named by a Dutch navigator aboard a Portuguese ship more than four-hundred years ago), to play several concerts. We were there at the right time, and got an invitation to perform for President Chiang Kai Chek's birthday party. What a thrill to play for all the dignitaries and the people of that beautiful country. The lush island located off the coast of China, has a fascinating history, some of it very brutal, having been claimed by several countries over hundreds of years. Eventually Formosa, now known as Taiwan, became part of mainland China. We may not have heard the last of *that* story.

Back in the Philippines, I was invited to a wedding for a cousin of our houseboy. I was asked to drive my big, black, shiny caddy and chauffeur the bride and groom from the church to the reception, and wherever else they wanted to go. The feasting on roast pig, lumpia (egg rolls), pansit noodles (transparent and delicious), and balut (fertilized duck eggs sixteen to nineteen days old), combined with so much laughing and dancing, made me feel part of the Filipino community, although I was halfway around the world.

Nearly twenty years had passed since I started my musical journey in England – with the determination to make it my life work. I was seeing a lot of the world *and* earning a living playing my horn.

33. Fourth Son

Nineteen sixty-six was greeted with some anxiety. At some point, we'd be reassigned back to the States. A fourth baby was due in February, and the many details of packing up a household, and moving a family of six to an unknown location, had to be contemplated. In the States we would be without the help of a housemaid; four little children under the age of six would be a handful, to say the least.

On February 18th, the band was given orders to travel to Baggio, a resort in the mountains of the Philippines. I was to be gone for five days but in the middle of a concert on the night of the 20th, I received a message that Miriam was taken to the hospital at Clark Air Force Base and that I should find a way back as soon as possible.

I caught the first bus out of town and arrived at Clark at two o'clock on the afternoon of the 21st, picked up the car, and hurried to the hospital. There in the nursery was our new little son. He seemed quite content and looked a lot like

Lal. We named him Sanjay Ragiv after India's Prime Minister Indira Ghandi's two sons, Sanjay and Ragiv.

Miriam was fine, and everything was already prepared at home. I took the usual pictures and primed the boys for the new little brother. I made sure the car was nice and clean, and we all piled in for the trip to the hospital to bring Mom and Sanjay home. He was a delightful baby, and his big brothers were excited and had a great time touching him.

If Miriam was disappointed in having another boy, she never expressed it. I felt great that we had four sons. In the Philippines, the people felt that it was good luck for families to have male children. They saw male children as more workers for the family. I did not share those sentiments. Children were my quest, whether boys or girls. In fact, I would love to have had at least two more. Children fill a house with happy faces, laughter, and fun.

I tried to make whatever sacrifice I could, so that the family would have an easier time. I never believed in, nor practiced, the concept of a percentage of duties or responsibilities between husband and wife. Miriam worked hard to keep the household running and the children cared for and it was a lot of work for her. Although I worked all day and often on weekends, I still tried to help out at home.

Lal, only sixteen months older than Sanjay, seemed to form a close bond with his new baby brother. Kris and Jaswan, three years apart, at times having rivalry over toys or activities, still got along fine. It was a joy to watch the four boys form a close and lasting companionship.

34. Colorado

The orders came to report to the 529th Air Force Band at Lowry Air Force Base in Denver, Colorado. As the boys frolicked and had the best of times, I tried to maintain priorities. Everyone had to get shots, physicals, and clothing for the colder weather that we would find in Denver. We sold the 1958 caddy for three times what the price would have been in the States. Today, that practice is more tightly controlled by the Filipino government.

The day finally arrived and all six of us got into a taxi and made it to the airport terminal. The flight was expected to take fourteen hours, and I knew just how difficult that could be with four little guys. I could have saved my worry. The three little boys climbed on board, and with the baby in arms, all four seemed like seasoned travelers. Before we lost sight of the base, they were all asleep.

I thanked my lucky stars that when we arrived at Travis Air Force Base, it was a bright, sunny afternoon. We had a bunch of luggage, no car, and four little boys all under the age of six. They all wanted to help carry things, even the baby reaching out. I got them into a taxi, went back to the town of Fairfield, missed our Mexican friends, and checked into a motel.

It was good to be back. The next morning, I went out shopping for a car. I found a Rambler station wagon and thought it was big enough to take us to Colorado. I brought the car to the motel and the boys gathered around and said, "That's great, Dad. Will it go fast?"

Once everyone got in, and the luggage was placed in the back and on the roof, I realized the Rambler was just barely large enough. Off we went into the July sun; destination Denver, Colorado. We drove about a hundred miles and a tire blew. I stopped on the side of a hill, changed the tire, and everything seemed pretty precarious. Eventually, we got another used tire and stopped for the night.

The second day found us traversing the hills and valleys of western Colorado. It was July, yet some of the mountain peaks were snow-capped. While the boys played and found funny things to laugh about, I said my silent prayers. The car was my main concern, but by late evening we saw the lights of Denver, and I breathed a sigh of relief.

35. Olive Street

The next morning, while Miriam watched the boys, I started my search for a place to live and got a rude awakening. Most landlords didn't want to rent to people with children or pets. I was getting desperate by the second day and, although the rent was extremely high, I secured an unfurnished apartment.

I rented a few pieces of furniture and borrowed some kitchen utensils from the base. I loved the fact, that even under trying circumstances, my boys acted like it was a big party. I signed into the base, enrolled Kris in Catholic kindergarten, and we settled down as best we could.

Soon the landlady stopped me and complained that the boys were climbing her trees. I could see the handwriting on the wall and began to look again for more suitable housing. In late September I found a perfect house with three bedrooms, and a fenced back yard; all for only ninety dollars a month. Ten days later we were moved in with all our furniture and even a new swing set in the back yard. Those were happy days for the boys.

I settled into my new band responsibilities. We were on call for every parade both near and far. I had no sooner gotten to Lowry Air Force Base than our band was called upon to play for The University of Denver Convocation on August 26, 1966. Lyndon Baines Johnson, President of the United States, gave the graduation address. I was playing music for one of the most influential people in the world – and I loved that President on top of it all.

The leaves began to fall and we prepared ourselves for the coming winter; the first real winter since we left Texas two years ago. Miriam needed a break. We'd been married ten years but the companionship and communication I had hoped we'd share had been strained and nearly broken by this time. We were isolated from family and friends who might have helped us overcome the stresses in our marriage. Miriam had not had the chance to visit her folks in Jamaica for several years – I hoped seeing them might help. I got her an airline ticket and, four days before Christmas, she flew home. I thought I knew what it was to work hard, but for the next five weeks a routine day went like this:

I was up at five-thirty in the morning, prepared breakfast for all four, one who was only ten months old, got the boys up at six-thirty, served breakfast, and fed the baby while the other three were eating. I'd go make sure the car was going to run. At seven-fifteen everyone got in the car. I dropped Kris at kindergarten, Jaswan at preschool at the base nursery, and Lal and Sanjay at the regular base nursery. Having delivered the boys to their respective places, I got myself to work before eight o'clock, played with the concert band, and did my other Air Force chores.

The return-cycle began at two-thirty in the afternoon. I dashed off to pick up Kris at kindergarten, Jaswan at preschool, and returned to the band room, parking the two boys in a room with some games to keep them occupied for the next two hours. I then played for Retreat at four-thirty and, as soon as the last note was played, I ran back to the room, picked up the two boys, and got the two little ones from the nursery. It was after five o'clock when we finally headed for home.

The baby was fed first while the older boys watch TV. I prepared supper, everybody ate, and watched more TV or played with toys. Before I did the dishes, I took care of the laundry and arranged clothing for the next day. Two boys were in cloth diapers, and the laundry was extensive. Sometimes I'd sneak off to the Laundromat and do the job so much faster than on the old wringer-type machine we had outside.

It was late January 1967, and Miriam came home. We were all glad to see her. I'm not sure how much longer I could have kept up with the daily chores, as I was wearing thin. She had a good vacation and seemed happy to be home with us.

I got the boys a puppy that they named Frisky. It was fun to watch them running around the backyard playing with their new friend. Miriam worked hard to teach the boys the alphabet and numbers. By the time kindergarten arrived, each could say his letters and count to twenty.

It was a sad day for all of us, in 1969, when the Air Force gave me orders to report to Kunsan Air Force Base in Korea, alone. We had been enjoying a time of peace and tranquility in our marriage, and fun as a family, and to have it broken up with the unexpected orders was almost more than we could bear. But as a member of the military, we have to go where we are sent. I gathered my wife and boys, and we knelt together in the living room and said a prayer. I then caught a midnight bus and began my long journey to Korea. I felt sick at having to leave my precious family.

36. Quest for Education

When I left Jamaica and joined the Royal Air Force, I had a sixth grade education from St. Catherine's Catholic School. The public schools, beyond sixth grade, were expensive. Without further education, there was little chance of securing a lasting job or career in my homeland.

For the first half of my career in the United States Air Force, I took the regular training classes that were required for my duties, but music still consumed my time and interest. Yet, in order to advance, I needed at least a high school diploma. So, in 1968, at the age of forty-four, I decided to earn a General Equivalency Diploma (GED).

I went to the education office at Lowry Air Force Base in Colorado and signed up to take the GED test – passing it the first time without any "bone-up" study. I attribute that to experience and to a great elementary education under the three nuns at St. Catherine's. I also read a lot. I had started reading "True Confession", "True Romance", and "True Detective" magazines. The stories held my interest, and my reading ability and comprehension grew steadily over the years.

After passing the GED so easily, I decided to register for my first college course in the summer of 1968. I took Political Science, made a "B" in that first class, and it wasn't as difficult as I'd expected. I was on fire for more education and I continued until I'd completed thirty hours.

I watched the boys in the evening using the later hours for study. Miriam decided she also wanted to go to school. We each took classes two nights a week, so the boys would have one of us at home.

On my assignment to Korea during 1971 and 1972, through the University of Maryland, I earned thirty more hours while I was alone and with little to do in my spare time. (Our band played for wounded troops from Vietnam, and for the troops stationed in Korea.) By the time I returned home, I had accumulated over sixty hours of college credit. I continued to go to school and take as many hours as possible.

I was transferred to K.I. Sawyer Air Force Base in Michigan and applied for educational leave so that I could finish college on campus. I only needed thirty credits to complete a degree, but it was necessary to take time out of the service. I was accepted into an Air Force program called "Operation Bootstrap" and was able to attend college full-time at Northern Michigan University in Marquette. I applied myself wholly to my classes and was not responsible for Air Force duties for fifteen months. What a break!

Graduation was on the glorious day of June 3, 1973. I wore a cap and gown. My whole family was there, all dressed up. The name Vincent Beach was announced, and I thought they were going to play "Hope and Glory" for me. My Bachelor of Science degree in Social Studies was earned. But my mother's old adage was remembered: *Don't throw away your stick till you cross the river.* I had only crossed the first river. There were more to come.

I had an overriding fear of being broke – without money – without marketable skills outside of music. I already had enough music experience to know that making a living in that arena in the civilian world was tenuous – *don't give up your day job* was a familiar saying. My mother and father were a driving force – instilling in us that one must make money – sacrifice at all costs, so that the family would be fed and clothed. There was no one to help if money ran out. Earning money in Jamaica was such hard work and every dollar carried great value. I felt that I had to do all I could to get as much education as possible so that, upon retirement from the Air Force, I could get a good job. To reach that goal was a cost that can never be calculated in dollars earned – I sacrificed my wife and children – unwittingly and without malice.

37. The American Dream

"Let's take a vacation. You guys have been so great to help me get this degree." We packed up, drove to Miami in our big Plymouth station wagon, and caught a plane to Kingston. The kids were tickled. We rented a condo through an old friend Verly, and spent two weeks in Kingston. The swimming and the beach were great, but the boys weren't used to seeing the grinding poverty of a place like Jamaica. They were saying, "Eeee yuck!" much of the time over unusual smells, poorly dressed people, and lots of garbage in the streets. We were able to visit our families and the boys got acquainted with their grandparents on Miriam's side of the family.

Back at K.I. Sawyer Air Force Base, in cool Michigan, it was soon time to pack again and take my new assignment at Tinker Air Force Base near Oklahoma City. I was so grateful for the Air Force programs which allowed me to get my bachelor's degree, and I felt I must continue to take advantage of all that was offered. I was accepted into the Master's Degree program in Psychology at Central State

University. The work was much more difficult than at the bachelor's level, and I was closing the books at three o'clock most mornings.

Miriam was also pursuing education and, having obtained her GED in Denver, decided to work on an Associate of Arts Degree. I admired the fact that she wanted to get further education. However, it was a huge hassle to try and arrange our schedules and also see that the boys were taken care of. I told her I would help her attain the degree and then return to my schooling. It was just too difficult for both of us to go at the same time. She earned her Associate's Degree and I resumed my studies.

I was motivated for the struggle because retirement from the Air Force was only a few years away. With a big family to support, and the desire for higher education for my boys, I was scared to death of ending up as a night watchman. So, once again, my studies went into high gear.

I drove the twenty miles round-trip each night to attend classes. My goal was to become a secondary teacher with a psychology background. The Air Force released me for six months so that I could take day classes and finish. After many nights shut up in the bathroom so that I could study, the big day came. On July 25, 1976, ten years after beginning my educational quest, I put on that cap, gown, and colorful stole, and walked proudly in the graduation procession. *Vincent C. Beach, Master of Education in Counseling Psychology.*

Just three weeks after celebrating America's bicentennial (two-hundredth) birthday, and playing in patriotic band concerts around Oklahoma, Texas and Michigan, the moment of graduation was packed with meaning for me. I was an immigrant who had taken hold of the opportunity offered in America, and was achieving the American Dream.

38. Go Faster, Dad!

I spent thirteen months at Kunsan Air Force Base, in Korea, during 1971 and 1972. Playing in concerts for the troops, the Korean people, and studying my college courses occupied my time. It was a joy to finally return home to my family.

Communication while away overseas was nothing like it is now. No easy telephone service, no e-mail, just trying to talk on a two-way radio crackling and interrupted. I very rarely was able to talk to Miriam or the children. I wrote nearly every day and she wrote to me to give me the news of home. The wives and children left at home to fend for themselves while Dad is out-of-reach, is a harsh reality. I hope that the military services are much more responsive today than they once were. Without the support of an extended family and an adequate income, life was difficult for my wife and boys.

I had spent a long tour of duty in Colorado, so orders were not unexpected when I returned from Korea. We bid farewell to the cozy home on Olive Street in Denver, and

145

headed for K.I. Sawyer Air Force Base in the upper peninsula of Michigan.

"Go faster, Dad, go faster! Dad, you're only going fifty miles an hour."

"There's snow out there, kids. I can't go any faster." All my little boys imploring, "Go faster, Dad." I was to hear that plea so often it was burned in my brain. I never drove fast enough to suit them.

In northern Michigan a lot of time had to be spent indoors due to deep snow and freezing cold. I tried to make a band like the Jackson Five. I got the boys started on instruments: Kris on the clarinet, Jaswan on guitar, Lal on drums, and Sanjay on the drum pad. I worked my hardest to get them interested, and we would go down in the basement and jam. There was nothing that pleased me more.

Kris had started piano lessons as a little boy in Colorado. He was in two recitals, but every practice was a struggle. Although he seemed to be playing well for a little kid, he cried over practice. I got a little girl from next door to practice with him, but he still quit. So I was trying once again.

Parents are often in a dilemma on how to direct their children's interests and abilities. I loved playing music and I wanted my children to enjoy it also. I think that music is a vital part of education because it truly is a universal language. Musical parents often have children who want to be active in music. Why my children had a lack of interest, I never understood, but I finally had to accept that fact and move on.

Spring and summer were the best up in northern Michigan. The boys learned to fish and we spent hours on the weekends trying to snag the big one. I threaded a lot of worms on a lot of hooks and it was pleasing to see the boys enjoy the outdoors.

In early 1974, the Air Force gave me orders to go to

Thailand for a twelve-month, unaccompanied tour. I was disgusted and alarmed that such an assignment would come so soon after Korea. I went to the Catholic Chaplain and laid out my fears for my wife and boys. He had nothing to offer. I talked to my superiors and tried to get the order changed. Miriam did not want to face being alone once more trying to take care of everything by herself. My pleadings fell on deaf ears, and I was reminded that my duty was first to the mission of the Air Force.

The whole family was crestfallen and apprehensive about the coming separation. I was on pins and needles hoping the family would be all right. Sadly, I had to leave.

I was fifty years old, the old man of the bunch at Utapoa Air Force Base, yet I made a lasting friend with a young airman in his teens named Gordon Kelly. We shared a dorm room and I would cook things for him. He still remembers that. Although I've never seen him again, we've talked on the phone and shared news over the years. I never ran after women or was unfaithful in any way to my wife like a lot of the men away from home. My time was filled with music, Air Force duties, and studies.

My being away from the family, and in a frozen place like Michigan, put added stress on Miriam as head of the household. The car was hard to start, the kids couldn't play outside a lot of the time, and all-in-all it was a *bad* duty station.

The discussion continues to this day revolving around the question from my sons: "Why were you gone all the time?" During the time that they were in the home, I spent a total of twenty-three months on two overseas assignments. Yet, to the family, it seemed that I was never there. As I began to pursue higher education with a vengeance, my time with my family became even less.

Upon my return from Thailand in 1975, we packed up

and left our base housing at K.I. Sawyer in Michigan and headed for my new assignment at Tinker Air Force Base, Oklahoma. As soon as we arrived at Tinker all I heard was, "Dad, we want motorcycles. You promised a long time ago." I bought three cycles. Kris and Jaswan each had his own, and Lal and Sanjay shared one. We went off each weekend to ride the trails and that was fun.

All four boys were playing baseball, competing with each other, and with all the other kids. Sports became the focal point of life. Although I'd never played competitive sports, beyond the playground soccer in Jamaica, I had four of the greatest sports enthusiasts imaginable. There went *my* dreams of a Beach Five.

39. No Diagnosis

Life was good for my boys. Everyone active, making friends, enjoying recreation activities at Tinker, and Kris hit his first golf ball. There was no sixth sense to tell us of impending disaster.

Early in 1976, Lal told us that he didn't feel well. I took him to the base doctor. The doctor couldn't find anything wrong but took lots of tests and kept him in the hospital for observation. The next day the doctor requested to see us. He asked, "Is your boy sexually active?" Needless to say, we were bowled over – an eleven year old sexually active? I thought that question over and thought he must be joking.

The doctor went on to explain that, from the blood work, they found the presence of antibodies which could indicate the possibility of syphilis, a sexually transmitted disease. The doctor wanted to know if we were infected. All of this blew my mind. Miriam and I were both tested and we had no trace of the disease. How could they arrive at such a conclusion?

As we found out later, there are antibodies present in the

blood of those with Lupus which can cause a falsely positive test for syphilis. Lal was given medication that seemed to help, but there was no diagnosis. There were good days and some not so good. He had joint pain, severe stomach pains, and rashes on his arms and shoulders. The symptoms would disappear one day, only to appear the next.

In the midst of the health problem with our precious kid, the Air Force issued another set of orders to return to Michigan. The news was greeted with whoops of joy, and we soon were on our way to Kincheloe Air Force Base located in the far north. The prospect of lots of fishing, golfing, and trekking around the woods helped the boys and us to cope with Lal's crisis.

On arrival at Kincheloe, I alerted the hospital that we had a sick boy with no positive diagnosis. We trooped back and forth to the military doctors but no one seemed to have an answer to Lal's medical problems. The months were filled with great concern.

40. Retirement

While at Kincheloe, and having already passed my twenty years of active duty, I was given an option: I could choose to be reassigned to McConnell Air Force Base in Kansas City, or I had to retire. If I chose Kansas, it was possible I could earn an additional stripe, which meant more money. I held a family conference and asked everyone's input. The boys didn't want to go to Kansas, nor did Miriam. Everyone agreed it would be best to accept retirement. The stay at Kincheloe was brief. Kris, as a junior in high school, was able to play on the school golf team during the spring of 1977. We moved back to my final duty station at Tinker Air Force Base in Oklahoma.

An officer in charge of personnel records had noticed there was an E-6 (five-striper) Tech Sergeant with two college degrees and he called to ask, "Sergeant Beach, why don't you apply to Officer Training School?"

"I'm too old. According to Air Force regulations, a guy can't be over thirty-five and I'm already fifty-two." The officer wrote to Washington, on my behalf, requesting an exemption from the age requirement. The reply came back that I was too many years past the cutoff.

I'd almost completed twenty-two years in the Air Force, I was armed with a Master's Degree in Education, I had my four growing super-sons, and it was time to fulfill the dream. We wanted to find a place to call home where we could buy a house, all be together, and not move anymore. While the boys were having a great time being back with old friends and familiar places, I spent a couple of months getting everything ready to retire.

The day of my retirement ceremony, which should have been exciting and memorable, ended as a disaster – one of the worst moments with my wife of twenty-one years. Problems had never been resolved and in one act of rage...I went to a morning meeting in my dress blues, and was followed home by several Air Force friends who were going to attend the final ceremonies. They were at the open door waiting for me, and I started to walk upstairs in our two-story house to get something. I heard a "whoosh" and felt a searing pain up and down my arm. Miriam had thrown a pot of boiling water at me. I was dumbfounded, embarrassed, and had no idea what to do. The boys were all there and I grabbed Kris and told him to take them and go on to the ceremony. I tried to act like nothing had happened, but I never felt so stupid. Wearing my wet jacket, I walked with my friends to the parade grounds to accept my awards.

Retirement had arrived and the ceremony was over. Life in the military was done. I know that Miriam was stressed and filled with fear of the uncertainties of retirement. I felt sickened for our life – there was no contentment. There seemed to be no answers and I didn't know what to do. I couldn't just leave her there. We had no idea what the next phase of our life, as the Beach family, would be like. We had already decided to go to Florida, so we packed, stored the large items, and traveled to Orlando.

We rented a small apartment, but felt ready to hit the road within the week. A white realtor buddy of mine (a former bandsman) showed us houses in all-black neighborhoods which were not of the quality we could afford. It seemed that we had too many children to live in the nicer neighborhood, and we were definitely too black (my friend finally confessed). Lal and Sanjay were enrolled in segregated schools, a new phenomenon for them, and they didn't understand. For the first time in their lives, the hate-filled words, "Hey, nigger" were directed at them.

The final insult seemed to be that I was too educated. I applied for a counselor position which, in part, would be to help college students select courses. "I'm sorry, Mr. Beach, I'm not sure you'd want this job because it only pays a little above minimum wage," stated the interviewer.

"With all due respect, you advertised that a counseling degree was required for the position," I replied, trying to maintain my composure. "Now, you're telling me I have *too many* degrees." The disappointment was beginning to mount, and I left with serious misgivings concerning our choice of Florida.

Miriam was the first to leave. She received a telegram with the news that her mother was dying in Jamaica and the family wanted her home. Discouragement was mounting and I was trying to decide what course of action to take when, out of the blue, I received a letter with the offer of a civil service job with the Bureau of Indian Affairs. I didn't need to think twice.

Kris flew with Lal and Sanjay back to Oklahoma City. Jaswan and I packed up the old Rambler and got out of Florida. He was tickled pink to be on a trip by himself with

Dad. We ate pizza, stopped at all the fast-food places we could, talked about planes and flying, and spent the night in a motel. As he was too young to drive, he went in the back of the station wagon whenever he wanted to rest. We had a lot of fun together in spite of the fact that we weren't sure what was next.

41. Transitions

Back in Midwest City, near Tinker Air Force Base, the trailer we had previously rented was vacant, and we moved in. I needed to go to Albuquerque for an interview with the Bureau of Indian Affairs. I left Kris and Jaswan with their friends, and took Lal and Sanjay with me.

Our trusty Rambler made the trip to the southwest, I passed muster in Albuquerque, and traveled to the Navajo Reservation in northeast Arizona. I found Ft. Defiance Agency, just north of Window Rock, and met Stan Milford, a Navajo, and Guidance Supervisor, who told me about the wonderful school where they needed a counselor. I also met Mr. Ernest Ingraham, the Assistant Education Superintendent, and we hit it right off. Stan would be my boss, but Mr. "I" would become my friend and mentor in a brand new career.

Toyei Boarding School, with eight-hundred Navajo children in grades kindergarten through eighth, was located sixty miles west of Gallup, New Mexico. The huge school, like a small city, was built on a great expanse of high desert pine, sage, and greasewood. There were comfortable houses to rent, at reasonable prices, in the government compound. A clinic with a registered nurse was located near the school entrance.

My beginning salary was twelve-thousand dollars a year when I accepted the position of Supervisory Guidance Counselor in October 1977. That was a huge raise for me. Within a few months the salary jumped to fifteen-thousand dollars. It was raining money. "Do they just give away money?" queried the boys. Weekly allowances were raised.

Miriam returned from Jamaica following the death of her mother, and as the older boys wanted to remain in Oklahoma, I thought it best to leave all four boys with her and get situated in the new job and environment. I made the sixteen-hundred-mile roundtrip nearly every two weeks. At Christmas, I drove to Oklahoma with a plan to move the family to Toyei.

The time of transition was far more difficult than I had anticipated. I don't think anyone wanted to move to Arizona and yet I had secured what seemed to me the best job of my life – at least the one with the biggest salary. I thought that I was putting the best interests of my family as foremost priority in that there would be plenty of money to take care of their growing needs. The decision I made had far-reaching consequences. I had already spent years studying extremely hard to get two degrees so that I could be assured of getting a good job. Then I was finding out that the education wasn't the sure bet I thought it would be. I wanted to get the family settled, buy the house they had always been promised and we had sacrificed for, but the scenario wasn't playing out as planned. In my quest for education, it seemed that I had, without intention, left my family behind. Following the transition to civilian life, my family was never truly together again. And for that, I must accept responsibility and the eventual consequences.

Kris was a senior in high school, Jaswan had good friends that he did not want to leave, Lal was in the seventh grade and Sanjay was in the sixth grade. Miriam left the family during Christmas of 1977 to carry out her own desires in life. I had a family meeting with the four boys and it was decided that Kris and Jaswan would stay with friends, but Lal and Sanjay would have to come with me. I loaded up my reluctant passengers and headed for Arizona and tried to make it a fun trip. I went back to work, and the boys registered in Ganado Public Schools.

The fifty mile round trip to school, in a bus filled with Navajo kids, got off to a shaky start. They didn't take kindly to having black students ride their bus and be in their classes. Taunts of "Zshenny, Zshenny" meaning black in a derogatory sense, in addition to other kinds of slurs, were endured. They called names, played dirty tricks, and there were daily fights. I felt so guilty that my boys were facing these unpleasant experiences. However, after a few weeks, a few of the Navajo students relented, and a little peace began to seep into the bus each day.

We were in the middle of the Navajo Reservation and medical help was far away for anything serious. I thanked God that whatever was wrong with Lal seemed to be in remission.

Within a few months Miriam had a change of heart. She decided that she would move to Arizona, help pull the family together, and make the new life that we had promised ourselves we would create after retirement from the military.

My official United States
Air Force portrait upon
completion of boot camp at
Samson Air Force Base in 1955

"To my Sweet Hubbie
from Princess" – 1957

Wedding Day in Jamaica – December 29, 1956

With my flute in the front row

Family photo in Denver – 1969

The Master's Degree is finally earned – 1975

PART FOUR
1977–1984

42. Arizona

The Navajo experience proved to be challenging not only for the boys, but for me as a black man. It took time for the Navajo employees and students to become accustomed to me. I endured the same racial slurs as the kids.

My title was Supervisory Guidance Counselor, but the actual work was quite different from being in an office counseling children. I was in charge of a large dormitory for fourth through eighth grade boys and girls. My job was to oversee every aspect of the care of kids who could not attend public school due to lack of roads or basic subsistence.

I had two Dorm Managers and twelve Instructional Aides under my supervision. I was unplugging vacuums which had sucked up large pieces of paper, searching for runaways in the middle of the night, and trying to make sure all the Navajo staff came to work, *and* on time. Little by little, I began to make my mark as a man who meant what he said, and also set a positive work example. The Navajos began to rely on me to help solve problems and to keep dorm-life moving along smoothly. The children came to me for help with personal issues or complaints. Best of all, the paycheck was great and I had time to read.

After Kris's graduation from high school and Jaswan's from ninth grade in June 1978, I went to Oklahoma and took the whole family to Toyei. We were together again, but none of the family wanted to stay there in the government housing – they felt isolated out on the Navajo Reservation. (Many families did survive well in the government employment and benefited from the opportunities of growing up in another culture.)

Williams Air Force Base was located near Chandler and that seemed to be the most convenient place to locate the family. Medical benefits were readily available as were many other retiree services. I moved Miriam, Kris, and Jaswan into a furnished apartment on the top floor of Eller's Upholstery Shop on Chandler Boulevard. I bought Kris an old yellow Ford, helped him enroll at Mesa Community College, and got him a monthly pass for the golf course at the base. Jaswan entered Chandler High School as a sophomore. I kept Lal and Sanjay with me at Toyei.

The rental was only temporary, and as everyone seemed to like Chandler, we decided to buy a house. On Buffalo Street in the south of Chandler, although nothing fancy, the dream-house had four bedrooms, a yard, an old evaporative cooler, and was close to everything including the schools. Out of my entire Air Force salary of ninety-thousand dollars for twenty-two years (and to the amazement of my sons) we had saved approximately thirty-three percent. We put ten-thousand dollars down on the house, and they moved in.

I continued to work at Toyei; traveling the five-hundred-mile round trip every two weeks. I brought their allowance, did the chores, home repairs, and serviced the several vehicles. As each son reached sixteen, that magic age of independence, he got a driver's license and an old car to go with it.

I never intended to be away from my family for so long. But, in spite of many attempts, I was never able to get a comparable job in the Phoenix area. The years slipped by and I missed so much of the day-to-day activities. I saw almost no sports involving my boys. I was not on hand for the daily help that is always needed and wanted by children and teenagers. And our marriage relationship further eroded. Yet, it was always a pleasure to come home on weekends and hear the boys talk about their accomplishments. They spent many hours with their friends making plans for glorious future goals: PGA, USAF, MD, and NFL. I later learned from my grown sons that they were determined, in spite of the negative circumstances that had beset our family life, to pursue those goals and let nothing or no one deter them.

43. Lupus

Perhaps due to the hot weather of the valley, Lal's illness manifested itself in a severe attack of pain and joint swelling. I took him to the hospital at Williams Air Force Base. The doctors referred him to St. Mary's Hospital in Phoenix and he was admitted. Two days later he was diagnosed with Systemic Lupus Erythematosus, a slowly progressive systemic disease that is marked by degenerative changes of tissues, skin lesions, arthritic changes, lesions of internal organs, wasting and fever. Wow!

The diagnosis left us bewildered. We'd never heard of Lupus. After he was released from St Mary's, we took Lal back to the base hospital. An old pediatrician took the case after talking with him. The doctor concurred with the diagnosis, and told us that he had some experience with the disease. Starting that day, he put Lal on a regimen of steroids, diet, and a lighter load of physical exercise. Those measures seemed to keep the disease in check.

Our sons were growing up well. On those weekends, twice a month, when I made the drive to Chandler, the five of us had a great time. We played golf and on Saturday nights we'd go to the Recreation Center on base and challenge Mr. Fuller, in the packed-with-junk yellow pants, to ping pong. Our goal was to beat that hot player. We tried to keep our close-knit relationship going in spite of my being an absentee dad. The most significant point to make is that the four boys remained companions, shared their friends, and challenged each other to be the best in their individual pursuits.

I spent the summers on educational leave, a program provided by the Bureau of Indian Affairs for continuing education. I took classes at Arizona State University, lived at home in Chandler, spent more time with the boys, and got my full pay. I used those years to take many educational administration courses which would prepare me for promotion within the Bureau of Indian Affairs or for another job in education.

44. Flight

Summers in Chandler were unbearably hot, yet our second son Jaswan could be seen day after day at Williams Air Force Base watching planes take off, and land. On the walls of his room were pictures of just about every plane that flew. He was a studious kid and knew what he wanted and how to go after it.

He was only fifteen years old, yet his knowledge of airplanes exceeded that of some of the men serving in the Air Force. He would meet and talk to every pilot and trainee that he could on the training base, and he could talk for hours about aircraft and flying. One kind officer arranged for him to have a ride in the jet simulator. His dream was to become an Air Force pilot.

During the fall of 1978, Jaswan enrolled at Chandler High School for his sophomore year. At about the same time, he registered for private pilot training. He logged many flying hours with an instructor and yearned for the day he could "solo". By the following spring, he was ready. He made his first solo flight and came in for a flawless landing. I stood watching this son of mine and I was filled with admiration.

The instructor gave him lots of praise for the flight, and Jaswan was overjoyed. Weekend after weekend he could be found at the little Chandler airport making short solo flights. The rental fee was sometimes beyond his allowance, but he saved his money and had at least one solo flight each month. He wanted to obtain a private pilot's license.

Before he could earn the coveted license, he was required to make a solo flight across state, including an instrument landing, and some night flying. He was more prepared than his instructor anticipated. The day came and, with confidence which belied his sixteen years, he climbed into the cockpit, went through his preflight checks, started his engine, reached the necessary pressure, and with a "thumbs up" to me, he was off down the runway into the bright blue sky. I stood there with awe watching my little boy pilot the plane, something I could not begin to do.

Setting his course for Tucson, he settled back and watched the clouds roll by. He said later that he felt at peace with himself and the world. This was what he'd wanted to do as long as he could remember. He landed and had the plane refueled while he grabbed a bite to eat. Within the hour, he was airborne and heading back to Chandler with all the joy in the world.

Before the end of winter 1980, the FAA was satisfied that Jaswan had shown enough flying skills. He was issued a private pilot license several months before his eighteenth birthday. That was a milestone and the next would be to secure an appointment to the United States Air Force Academy.

During his junior year in high school, Jaswan began an intense quest for the Academy. He went out for football and track. He worked ceaselessly to get fit. At the break of dawn, he was at the weight room to work his body into shape. By the fall of 1980, he was a robust young man, six feet tall and weighing one-hundred-sixty-five pounds. He was number "88" on the football squad. He felt confident and had already received favorable responses, including official visits, to his application to enter the Academy.

45. Wings of the Dawn

Jaswan graduated from Chandler High School in 1981. His hard work and persistence had earned him a scholarship to the United States Air Force Academy. He was to enter the Air Force Preparatory Academy for one year to build up some deficiencies in math. He was going to Colorado Springs – the cadet's blue uniform would soon be his.

He carefully packed his bag, said his goodbyes to his mother and brothers, and I drove him to the Academy. He was excited and also a little apprehensive. He didn't put his feelings into words, but it seemed that his expectations weren't exactly met. His first stop on campus was the dining room where the cadets had to enter with precision steps; stand until told to sit, eat when told to eat. That may have been the cause for his feelings coupled with leaving home for the first time. He was assigned a room and a roommate and, as he was a well-disciplined young man, took to the military aspects of his training.

He came home for Thanksgiving and Christmas and remarked each visit that he was studying twice as hard just to keep up. The math was difficult, but he was resolved to do everything in his power to hang on. He wanted us to know that if he wasn't able to make it, that he had done the very best he could. He enjoyed Christmas and returned to the Academy.

In January, while preparing for the semester exams, he realized there was no way he could bring his math grades up to the "C" requirement, so he resigned and came back home to Chandler. He immediately enrolled for the winter semester at Mesa Community College and was doing well in his courses. He decided to work towards a degree in engineering with one thought in mind; to graduate from college and enter the Air Force pilot training program.

Around October of 1982, we noticed that Jaswan was losing weight. Having never been sick in his whole life, he thought maybe he'd been studying too much. He never complained, but the weight loss became more pronounced. On Christmas Day, we had our dinner at Williams Air Force Base and played our usual family golf tournament, but he said he didn't want to play; he'd just walk along.

In January 1983, for the first time, he said that his stomach hurt and that he felt congested. I took him to the base emergency room and they gave him medication to settle his stomach and prescribed a vaporizer for his nasal congestion. However, he had suffered serious weight loss and once more we went to the doctor and they took X-rays and blood tests. The X-ray showed nothing and the results of the blood tests were yet to come.

By the middle of February, the strong and healthy son of ours seemed to be deteriorating fast. We took him to the base hospital and he was admitted with an initial diagnosis of leukemia. He was put in isolation for fear of infection. As I watched him lying in that hospital bed, it tore at my heart, and I questioned all that we had done. Two days later he was transferred to St. Mary's, one of the major hospitals in Phoenix (where Lal was diagnosed with Lupus), for closer observation and a more positive diagnosis.

We sometimes perceive doctors as having magical powers to diagnose and cure. Great frustration occurs when we realize doctors are mortal and don't have all the answers. At St. Mary's, doctors of all specialties gathered around our son's bed. They poked, felt, took blood, gave shots, transfusions, put him on oxygen, but none was ready to attempt a diagnosis.

When a doctor inquired about our family history, Miriam told him about Lal having Lupus. The following day, Jaswan was diagnosed with Acute Systemic Lupus Erythematosus. The diagnosis did not scare me as I had been seeing Lupus in its milder form with Lal for several years. Jaswan was placed on high doses of steroids which can be devastating to the kidneys. He was given a blood transfusion that raised his temperature to one hundred-five degrees. The trial-and-error medical treatment continued while he lay there apparently in pain, but uncomplaining.

Five days after being admitted, he was released. The following day Jaswan was up bright and early, gathered his books and was off to his college classes. The next day he didn't feel well enough to go to school and he stayed in bed all day. By now I was back at Toyei, worried sick, but hopeful that since a diagnosis was made, he would begin to recover.

But later that day, he was having difficulties walking and may have been in severe pain – still uncomplaining. The night of February 24, 1983, Jaswan walked out to the living room where Kris and Sanjay were meeting with Mitch, the Baptist youth minister their mother had invited to visit with the boys. Jaswan, coming from the hall said he, too, wanted to accept Jesus. Sanjay's Christian testimony evolved from the experience of that evening.

No one called me, but I knew he was sick and I wanted to check on him. Work was over at ten o'clock that night and I jumped in my old Chevy and headed for Chandler. Not having a house key, I climbed in the window and heard a groan and wheezing coming from Jaswan's room. I went to his room and asked, "How do you feel? What's going on?" His breathing was severely labored and I reached for the inhaler and it proved useless.

He said, "I don't feel so good. And I need to go to the bathroom." I helped him and waited.

Jaswan seemed to be slipping fast; sensing the urgency of the situation, I helped him into his clothes to make a trip to the emergency room. He turned to me and said, "Let's wait awhile."

I replied, "Okay, tell me when you're ready."

Within a few minutes he said, "Let's go now."

I picked him off the bed and half-carried him to the car. No one was awake and I let that be. Twenty minutes later, he was wheeled into the emergency room at Williams Air Force Base.

The doctor on duty had been asleep but he took one look and, alarmed, said, "You have a very sick boy here." I stood there helpless and watched the doctor and nurses try to revive him. Every few minutes he would respond to the medication and, no sooner, he would fade away again.

Around six o'clock that morning, I called home and told them the sad news: Jaswan was struggling for his life. Miriam arrived with some friends and held a prayer meeting in a small room. By eight o'clock there were doctors everywhere doing all that they could do to keep him alive.

I went in to see what they were doing and this handsome, once vibrant son gave me the "thumbs up" sign as if to say, "Don't worry, Dad, it'll be okay."

At eight-thirty the doctors asked me to sign permission to operate. A helicopter was called to evacuate him to intensive care at St. Mary's, but he was too sick for the move. At ten o'clock the doctors continued to work feverishly, but the answer now seemed to be only in the power of prayer. In my heart I said, "Lord, I pray take away this bitter chalice, but if this is Thy will for Jaswan, then Thy will be done."

At ten fifty-six the morning of February 25, 1983, I looked at the lifeless body of Jaswan. He was nineteen years, nine months, and nineteen days old. He lived for such a short while and yet he seemed to have accomplished more than some of us who have lived a lifetime. We ask: *Why?* We must realize that we are not given a contract stating how long a life we will have and, therefore, we should be prepared that death can come at any time.

Three days later, Jaswan was buried near a tall pine tree at Queen of Heaven Catholic Cemetery in Mesa. A large group of friends and classmates gathered at the graveside service to give Number 88 a last farewell.

The autopsy report that arrived several weeks later gave the cause of death as Acute Systemic Lupus Erythematosus, which affected his kidneys, heart, and lungs. His organs failed from the effects of the disease as well as the medications used for treatment of a little-known illness – particularly in its acute form.

Jaswan's death reminded us how vulnerable we *all* are. The Book of Life was brief for him – he didn't know how many pages were in his book, but we believe that he made the most of every day that was given to him. His life was well-lived – he pursued his goals, he had great friends, and he loved his brothers. We knew he was safe in the arms of God.

If I rise on the wings of the dawn, if I settle on the far side of the sea, even there your hand will guide me; your right hand will hold me fast. Psalms 139:9–10

46. Sanjay's Testimony

Sanjay, my youngest son, shared his recollection of the last night of Jaswan's life and the impact it has had on his own life to this day.

The night before my brother Jaswan died, my oldest brother Kris and I were sitting in the living room of our Chandler home. Jaswan was sick and had been lying in bed for a couple of days. My mother, who had been attending the First Baptist Church on Ray Road for a few months, invited the youth minister, Mitch, over to talk with us.

We were a little put off by this invitation, but Mitch knocked on the door, and we let him in. He was friendly and we were shooting the breeze with him for a little while. My mother was with Jaswan in his room putting cold towels on his head and trying to comfort him.

We turned off the TV and the talk turned serious. "What do you think about God?" Mitch asked. Kris and I looked at each and we didn't know exactly what to say. So we asked a few questions. Mitch explained who Jesus Christ is and about Easter and the Resurrection. He asked if we knew what it was to be a Christian. Well, we weren't sure of that either, so he explained that God sent Christ, His Son, to bridge the gap between humanity and Himself. After some more explanation, he asked, "Do you want to accept Jesus Christ?"

We both said, "Yes." And just before we got ready to pray, we looked up and saw Jaswan walking down the hall.

He said, "What're you guys doing?" Mitch replied that he'd been explaining the Gospel to us and we were getting ready to pray a prayer to accept Jesus Christ as our Lord and Savior.

Jaswan said, "Well, I want to do that." Jaswan knelt down with us and Mitch went through the sinner's prayer. As we were getting up, Jaswan pushed himself up with a hand on my shoulder. It was a struggle, and I was struck by how weak he seemed to be. He walked back to his room to lie down.

Mitch chatted with us about attending church and then he left. Mom was back with Jaswan taking care of him, and we finally went to bed. When I got up to go to school, I looked in his room and Jaswan wasn't there. I went on to school and at ten-thirty I remember looking at the clock in my classroom, deciding I'd go home for lunch.

Kris hadn't gone to school, so we were both there when Mom came in crying and told us that Jaswan had died. Personally, I made a deal: "God, I'm going to read the Bible everyday from start to finish and if it doesn't make sense to me, I'll let it go."

That last night of my brother's life has become part of my Christian testimony which I often share. I was so grateful that Mitch came and showed us "The Way" and that in my brother's last hours, he had peace. That's been with me always.

I've been able to understand life a lot better and believe that the most important thing is to live each day centered in Jesus Christ.

47. Divorce

That Monday evening – following the farewell for Jaswan – Kris, Lal, Sanjay, and Jay Johnson (one of their best friends) were gathered in our living room. Everyone was feeling terrible. A blow had been struck that was totally unexpected and no one knew what to do. I talked with them as best I could to let them know that life must go on; they had to carry on with their activities and not let this tragedy derail them.

The end was in sight for our marriage which had grown increasingly strained. I didn't know how it would end, but it seemed that reconciliation was impossible by this time. It was as if each person in the family of six was involved in his or her own self-preservation and the family had ceased to function as a unit. I had been away from home for six years, coming only on two weekends a month. My leadership was questioned at every turn; my motives for working far from home were criticized, and I myself was wondering why I was so far away and had not even been able to prevent the death of our beloved son.

Miriam stayed in her bedroom following the burial and, when I tried to talk with her about the loss to our family, her only comment was, "Don't think that this will change anything." I didn't know what she meant until a few days later.

I had mailed a letter written February 13, 1983 to Miriam; an appeal and attempt to explain my feelings towards our life. The letter was still in the mailbox when Jaswan died and I retrieved it and put it in my briefcase where it has remained these many years. The letter detailed my blame towards her, but in looking back I know that I had failed to be there for her over many years of our life. The quest to improve my education, and the chance to secure a well-paying job, had obscured the emotional needs of my wife and children.

Our next door neighbor, perhaps in sympathy for what had happened to Jaswan, gave me a six-month-old buff-colored cocker spaniel puppy named Sir Ralph. He had been unable to sell the puppy, and I gladly accepted his gift. Taking my new little friend Ralph, I had to leave my boys and head back to work at Toyei. Now I had someone to retrieve my golf balls as I hit the shag bag out into the field. He ate what I ate; usually stew. He was joyful just to be with me. He rode in the car with me wherever I went. His tail, which had not been bobbed, would turn in a circle like a windmill when he ran. Ralph remained my funny little companion for almost sixteen years.

The day I returned to Toyei, from the funeral, the sheriff from Keams Canyon knocked on my door and asked, "Are you Vincent Beach?"

"Yes, and what can I do you out of?" I replied.

"I have a warrant for your appearance." I looked at the paper and it was a divorce petition filed by Miriam. The letter I had written, but which was never read, would have made no difference. It was too late.

We went through the sorry process of lawyers and equitable distribution. She was awarded the house and all its contents. My only legal responsibilities were to support Sanjay who was under eighteen, and provide half of my military retirement to her each month. The bitterness and upheaval caused by the divorce added to the boys' trauma at losing their brother. Divorce, in the eyes of our sons, had always been viewed as intolerable.

We had many conversations trying to find a way to put what had happened into perspective. The events had been extremely disturbing. From that time forward, I would stay in a room at Williams Air Force Base when I came down for weekends. The boys and I would still do our activities of golf and go to the Recreation Center. Each of us, in our own way, tried to pick up our life and move on.

48. Three Grown Sons

Weekends were a lonely time that fall of 1983. I would go into Holbrook to do my laundry and to play a round of golf. Ralph rode in my old, olive-green 1974 Chevy four-door RAF 222 to keep me company. I smoked my pipe, wore my baseball cap, and would settle back for the eighty-mile ride to that dusty, barren little country town. Although I used to attend Catholic Mass at Keams Canyon while at Toyei, I no longer went to Mass because tee-time conflicted with Mass-time.

The most fun I had during those months was when Kris, my oldest son, would come to visit. He'd graduated from Arizona State University in December 1982. After working at Chandler High School coaching track during the spring, he took his first teaching job at Red Rock Day School in the Shiprock Agency of the Navajo Reservation. Both of us were working for the Navajos. Rather than live in government housing, Kris bought himself an old motor home to live in at Red Rock. He would fly down Route 666 and come to visit his "old man" on weekends. We would then take off to Gallup and play golf and have a bite to eat. He would tell me stories of his funny experiences as a P.E. teacher in his new job. He had a huge head of curly black hair worn Afro-style. He was tall and strong and ready to make his move towards the PGA.

I kept telling him, "You can't climb a mountain with extra baggage." We had heated conversations on the fact that he wanted his girlfriend Ruth to come and live with him in Shiprock. Ruth, although eighteen, had not yet graduated from high school, but Kris felt he'd found the ideal mate. It seemed to me that he should first work to get on the PGA which had been his ultimate goal for several years. He was a highly accomplished golfer by this time and well-admired by local golfers.

"I can do it," was his steady reply. So at the end of his first year of teaching, he left the school and went to live in his motor home with Ruth on the streets of Chandler. They worked at small jobs and kept themselves afloat. I still supplied his pass to Williams Air Force Base so he could practice golf, and gave him a small allowance. We would meet up once in awhile on weekends where I stayed at the base, and we'd have good meals at the NCO Club, or go into Chandler and pick up Lal and Sanjay and eat at our favorite joint, The Golden Bamboo Chinese Buffet on Alma School Road.

Sanjay still lived at home with his mother and was in his senior year at Chandler High School. A football star and very popular young man, he seemed to be thriving. Scholarship offers were coming in. I saw him win the state championship in the hundred-meter dash – a breathtaking race in which he beat Ruth's equally talented brother, John Fields.

Lal still stayed at his mother's house when he came home on weekends from the University of Arizona. At nineteen, his health seemed to be holding steady although he was still under the watchful eye of the base pediatrician.

But the disturbing events of 1983 – the death of his brother and the divorce and bitterness – began to manifest problems for Lal. He was not as enthused about school as he had once been. He complained about his car, so I got him a fast little Triumph. He used to brag that it got him home from Tucson in an hour going "ninety miles an hour."

His grades began to slip and he began to spend more time with weight-lifting than with his studies. He joined the University of Arizona's body-building club and, with a fearless heart, embarked on a regimen of power-lifting and body-building. His five-foot-six-inch frame began to fill out and muscles developed to show a well-defined body on this handsome young man. Throughout his younger years he had been unable to compete in organized sports, except for golf. Weight-lifting, as he was practicing it, was in direct defiance to the need for restraint in physical activities as part of the control of Lupus. I had to admit he was a great sight to behold, and watching him in tournaments was quite a thrill. Although I knew the inherent danger of what he was doing, he was strong in his conviction that he was going to live and do what he wanted for as long as possible. I had to respect his desire and support him in his efforts.

I went with Lal to Sanjay's 1984 graduation from Chandler High School. My last son made it through high school, and it was a proud moment. Sanjay had secured a full scholarship to Colorado State University for football. There was my kid, who wore corrective lenses, and had undergone eye surgery as a young boy, ready to make his way as a wide receiver. I knew so little about the game of football but, from that time, I became an avid fan.

I loved my sons with all my heart and felt that I had raised them the best that I knew how. Yet, each in turn, found fault and freely expressed themselves in the conversations around the table. The recurring theme was that I had been gone "all the time – that I wasn't there for them." I listened to them and felt that I had to endure their castigations and blame, because I somehow deserved them. In my mind, I had done all I could to see that they got an education and an upbringing that helped them to seek whatever they wished to pursue in life.

I was fifty-two years old when I retired from the Air Force in 1977, a black man, and unable to secure employment commensurate with my education in the civilian world. I had "veteran's preference" in government hiring and took the first job I was offered, and did my best to climb the career ladder in the Bureau of Indian Affairs. I was aspiring to be a principal and indeed, within a few years of being at Toyei Boarding School, I was detailed as Acting Principal several times. I had to be available and on the job – I felt I couldn't drive the five-hundred mile round-trip to Chandler whenever there was an activity. I missed all of the graduations, except for Sanjay's, and most of the sporting events. Looking back, I wonder at myself how I missed so much.

I am reviewing all that I did and didn't do in an attempt to find an answer as to why my sons were critical and our closeness lost. It seemed like every member of our household was looking out for themselves and what would best serve their own needs rather than for the overall benefit of the family unit. I had a good job at Toyei Boarding School and we could have made our life right there – the family chose to leave and so I bought the house in Chandler. Prior to that time in 1978, I had always lived with them and was only gone the two times the Air Force sent me overseas on unaccompanied tours. Had there been a loving relationship with my wife, I believe we would have found a way to all be together.

49. A Letter from my Heart

To know that you have caused hurt to another person is a nearly-intolerable feeling. Only in the writing of my story have I been forced to review my actions and wonder how I could have short-changed my family while at the same time believing that all I was doing was for them. These words are for Miriam:

I did not deal you a fair hand. What I should have done, I didn't do. There was unexpressed love which you were denied in your younger years. I could have stood there and said, "I love you" a thousand times – I should have said it, for I felt it. People live together and often the careless words become the catalyst for a quarrel. People forget that this is the same person that you loved yesterday.

There are enough mistakes to go around, but I want to see you in the light of the girl I once loved. You were my princess, my queen. How can one say that there was no love when two people lived together, had children, and struggled through adversity? I can't honestly say that I felt loved, but then I can't say that I knew what love was supposed to be like. I thought that love manifested itself in acceptance. I thought that was love and didn't know that there was a depth that I had missed. I thought that love (by that I mean acceptance) should have produced joy and unity between the two of us. But we didn't find the expression that was necessary for a complete and happy relationship.

I thought if I just showered you with everything that you needed physically, that was enough. You were left emotionally wanting. I really didn't know better. My upbringing in the language of love was very short. My father and mother were respectful of each other, and worked side by side, but I never heard or saw affection as one might expect between husband and wife.

In the twenty-six years of our married life I never tried to hurt you willfully, although unkind words were said in the heat of an argument. You worked hard to care for the four boys and you were often alone in that chore.

I regret with all my heart that we were not able to make a lasting, loving relationship. You will have my respect forever, and I will leave it now in the hope that you will forgive me.

*Jaswan at the United States
Air Force Academy – 1981*

*Lal graduates from
Chandler High School
with honors – 1982*

ARIZONA STATE UNIVERSITY
Commencement
December 17th, 1982

Kris earns his diploma from Arizona State University – 1982

Sanjay graduates from Chandler High School – 1984; received a full scholarship in football at Colorado State University from 1984–1988

Three grown sons on Father's Day – Sanjay, me, Lal, and Kris

PART FIVE
1983–Present

50. Kinlichee Principal

Six years into my new career as a Supervisory Guidance Counselor, my old friend Mr. Ingraham, Assistant Education Superintendent for Ft. Defiance Agency, recommended me for the position of principal at a run-down, problem-ridden, old-time boarding school called Kinlichee. Located at seven-thousand feet above sea level, seven miles east of Ganado, a mile-and-a-half off highway 264 on a gravel road, down a steep, dirt hill, nestled in a picturesque valley of red-rock formations, pine and sage, lay my destiny for the next three years.

I had been sent there earlier as an interim principal to try and keep the school afloat during a time when the powers in Washington, D.C. were threatening closure. (The government was trying to reduce the number of Navajo schools under the control of the Bureau of Indian Affairs. This was accomplished by closing schools and forcing the states to provide public education for the Navajo children, or turning the schools over on a contract-basis to local control.) I had received a glowing Letter of Commendation from Phillip Belone, Agency Superintendent of Education in Ft. Defiance, stating in part, "Since you have been detailed to Kinlichee, the total attitude of the school board has become very positive, in that, we have finally developed a working relationship with the school board." That sounded great, and I was pleased with the compliment.

I was hired in August 1983 as Principal. With a staff of forty personnel, both Bureau of Indian Affairs (civil service) and contract (under control of the local school board), and a school board which had a large measure of control over the affairs of the school, I had my work cut out for me. Yes, even for an old, retired, experienced Air Force man like myself.

My marriage of twenty-six years was over, my son had died; nothing I had done stopped either disaster, and I needed the new challenge to fill my days and nights. It was time for me to move on – I accepted the appointment and gave up my secure civil service status to go under the new contract salary schedule, which boosted my income and grade. I was now the equivalent of a GS-12 and earning for me, big money; thirty-one thousand dollars a year. I was assigned the "White House," the newest and best house on the compound, which had been built for a previous principal.

I moved my several footlockers into the unfurnished house and borrowed a bed, table, and chairs from Toyei Boarding School – Lorraine Lewis gave me a ragged old brown couch – a white sheet hung at the picture-window. I had a few favorite cooking utensils and my golf clubs.

In that remote place, I found a group of Navajos, most of them old-timers in the Bureau of Indian Affairs, who were cooperative, and for the most part, congenial. Combined with them was a group of characters, both black and white, who came from all parts of the United States to teach Navajo children. They came and went with regularity (I remember one white teacher who stayed one night, and without a word of farewell or explanation, was gone by morning.)

I was under the supervision of a recalcitrant school board. When I was hired to direct the school, the positive attitude for which I had received a commendation, was over. At times it seemed that "payoff" was the only way to get what I needed for the school. I refused, forgot about diplomacy, and often butted heads with the members. Mr. Ingraham would travel over to Kinlichee and smooth the waters of discontent for all of us.

By September, school was in full-swing. The enrollment was far below what was required to maintain the number of staff on hand. The budget that I directly supervised was small. I had two office personnel; Johanna Begay, the secretary, who had been there for years, and Lorraine Lewis who I hired from Toyei to help me with the budget. Ralph, my sidekick-puppy, came to work with me each day and sat under my desk.

Soon after school started, I got a call from Mr. Ingraham. "Vincent, I have an experienced Homeliving Specialist here that I want you to get on your staff. She can be a big help to you out there," he stated.

"I can't afford to have her," was my emphatic reply.

"Well, you can't afford *not* to have her. She's the best." I reluctantly agreed to meet with the woman and introduce her to the school board.

I must confess that when "The Best" showed up, I was somewhat less than friendly. I didn't want a high-priced employee on my endangered payroll. But she was friendly and easily won over the school board (who knew her boss Leonard Arviso, one of the movers of the Navajo Reservation). Joe Mateba, always a positive man, smiled and said, "Well, if she's good enough to work for Leonard Arviso, she's good enough to work for us."

Mr. Ingraham was right. Between the two of us, and a willing staff, we began to turn little Kinlichee into an oasis of education, beautification, and discipline for all.

51. Flag Ceremony

*S*orrow is *Bourne in a Hasty Heart*; I looked at that sign I had penned on a piece of yellow legal paper and taped to the wall behind my giant, gray-metal government desk. Each day I had to remind myself of the truth of that statement as I dealt with unruly staff and kids.

"Mr. Beach, Clifford's calling names and he won't go to class," reported a teacher. I went and tucked nine-year-old Clifford under my arm and hauled him into Miss Weaukie's fourth-grade class.

"Mr. Beach, the van won't start; it's too cold," reported Robert Shirley, the kindergarten bus driver. Those tiny kids had to be transported long distances over sometimes impassable (or should I say impossible) roads to school each day. They were no longer allowed to stay in the dorms at such a young age. In my warm parka, I'd go out on many freezing mornings and help Robert get the vehicle started.

"Mr. Beach, I have a secret to tell you," little Eric Wilson said as he whispered in my ear. It wasn't a big secret, but I had an open-door office housed in what used to be the isolation room of the dormitory wing. Children had free access, although Johanna tried to intercept them from her desk by the door.

"Hello, Mr. Beach. You need to turn in your budget by five o'clock today. The Superintendent wants to see what's going on out there," giggled a female voice over the phone from Ft. Defiance. I would have to drop everything and turn my attention to the mountain of paperwork and budget details (before computers). Had Lorraine Lewis not been efficient, I would never have made the many short-notice deadlines and requests.

I held a teacher's meeting each Monday. I was trying to make sure the curriculum was followed. I was trying to put a halt to candy sales which appeared to be for private gain, rather than the good of the school. I was trying to help create an education team based on what was *best* for the children.

"Mr. Beach, these kids just run off to school trying to beat each other to the door, yelling and screaming. They get to class in total disorder." The new Homeliving Specialist was starting to take charge of the dorm which housed the first through sixth grade boys and girls. Together we decided to have a morning flag ceremony and march them to school. But first the old flag pole which had fallen down needed to be put back in place.

With Juan Curley, Tommy Manning, Robert Shirley and me pushing and shoving, we got the rusty old pole back in the ground. We invited the Navajo Chairman to join us for a flag raising ceremony, but the Vice Chairman Edward Begay came instead. It was a glorious moment out in our dirt-covered courtyard. A podium was set up to hear the words of encouragement and support. Our Boy Scout troop, in their smart uniforms, marched out with the brand new flag and it was raised. Juan Curley, one of the few male Instructional Aides and a veteran, had taught them how to do it properly.

From then on, every day before school, all the children lined the walks on either side of the dorm. They stood at attention, hands over hearts, as the phonograph issued forth the marches of John Phillip Sousa, and the flag was raised. The Pledge of Allegiance was led by one of the staff, although I was always present. Then we walked the children to the classroom building. What might seem like a small step was the beginning of routine and discipline which helped to bring our troops into order.

52. Crossroads

In November 1983, life at Kinlichee was beginning to settle down to a routine. I spent most of my hours at the school. I'd go home for a little warmed-up stew which I shared with Ralph. A dog named Sylvia, silvery-white, with a black-patch over one eye, and belonging to the Homeliving Specialist, would be waiting for me beside Ralph on my front porch. I began to feed her along with Ralph.

Then the three of us would chip on back down to the dorm for the evening activities. These were fun times. The kids would gather around and talk. Wednesday was "Movie Night" and I'd get the 16mm projector out and put on a rented movie on those big reels. Videos had not come to Kinlichee. We'd have a good cowboy story or children's movie that had been requisitioned in the summer and came in the mail. The community was invited to attend for fifty-cents a head.

I ran the canteen out of a closet in the dorm living room and made quite a bit of money for school extras. Once in awhile I'd have to go outside and get rid of someone causing trouble by having too much to drink. But the school was like having one big family to look after and it occupied my time well.

I still was not very friendly with my Homeliving Specialist. In fact, I was very rude one day questioning where she had gone with her special education class, which was also one of her assignments. "Where have you been?" I said in a very gruff manner. She explained that she'd taken the kids to watch some excavation work being done. I chastised her further about her responsibilities, and I heard later that she cried to Nora Tso, the Dorm Manager.

I felt somewhat chagrined about my behavior. That night I picked out some of my very cool record albums and took them to the dorm. She had a phonograph in her office and, with the children all gathered around, we listened to Paul Horn play his flute and Charlie Parker play his sax. That was a breakthrough in working together more harmoniously. I could see she was working hard and earning her salary.

I began calling her "Catrin," my Jamaican lingo for Cathryn. For several months we worked hard to bring new life to this small, but vital school. I hired an experienced librarian, Carl Cushman, and with special monies, we got new books and Carl set about making a library. Then, wonder of wonders, we got six Apple computers. We were really "uptown" and Carl knew how to get them up and running.

We converted an old metal shed into a very small gym. Our resident sports buff, Marlene Davis, got two Wolverine basketball teams organized. They looked terrific wearing their bright red and white uniforms. Clubs were formed and all the kids got to be in a club and "Club Night" was a time of great fun. I ran a little instrument club after gleaning a bunch of old cast-offs from Shiprock Agency. My group learned to blow a few notes.

It was brilliant watching this entire school and staff

start to shine. Christmas came and the kitchen staff baked three-hundred-and-fifty big gingerbread boys. A hand-made Navajo Nativity scene designed by Marlene Shondee graced our courtyard. New trees were planted, fencing put up (Navajos do not generally care for fences) and we tried to grow grass.

I got a call from Ft. Defiance Education Office with a demand to make an inventory of all equipment in the newer parts of the school, as well as Old Main (the original hand-cut, red-stone building typical of Navajo Reservation school architecture of the 1930s). I had only the weekend to complete the work, and "Catrin" said she'd help me. We went through every building that Saturday, March 3, 1984 with her calling out ID numbers on equipment, and me checking them off on the inventory sheets. I began to have a funny feeling.

When we were finished, we went back to the office and personal conversation took place for the first time. We found out each was no longer married. We talked about our families. With a sudden inspiration, I ran to look at the calendar to find a date and said, "Would you like to go to Gallup and play golf?"

She thought that over and said, "Sure. That sounds fun although I don't know how to play golf at all." As is often the case, I had just arrived at a crossroads without forethought, map, or plan. Whichever way I chose to travel, the course of my life could change forever.

I had worked side by side with the Homeliving Special-ist for several months, fed her dog, and walked up the stone path with her each night at nine o'clock. She lived across the road from me in her little apartment. I'd never thought of her in a non-professional way, nor did I know anything about her personal life. I was about to break the strict rule I'd made for myself – to *never* fraternize with the employees.

I had kept true to that all through the years, even though there had been some opportunities to do otherwise.

My head began spinning. *What was happening?* I called her up on the phone and said, "What's going on?" And we talked and talked, and she was feeling the same way. We hadn't really stopped and looked at each other. All we did was work on the school. But that *mysterious force* of love was taking over.

Wednesday, March 7, 1984 was a day to remember. Kinlichee was hosting the Agency principals' meeting, a big deal for our small school. School Superintendent Charles Johnson was coming, as well as Mr. Ingraham, and ten principals from far-flung areas. "Catrin" helped me get everything organized and was hostess for the day. She looked cute wearing a velvet skirt, vest, and two long, dark-brown ponytails. I was *Mr. Cool Principal* in my dark blue sports coat and Air Force tie. I felt like I had reached the pinnacle of success in my Navajo experience.

That evening, after all the kids were settled into their activities, I took my Homeliving Specialist in the government vehicle, down the old dirt road, to attend the Kinlichee Chapter Meeting and make a public relations appearance. On the way home, I stopped the vehicle out on the wild and lonely road and gave her a nice, regular kiss. "I've been wanting to do that all day," I smiled. We got home and eventually bid good-night.

As soon as she got in the door of her apartment, I called her on the phone and sang, just like Perry Como:

And I love her so, the people ask me why, how I come to know, I tell them I don't know. I guess they'll understand how lonely life can be and life began again the day you took my hand...

I began to call her AC, the initials for Ann Cathryn, and we most likely didn't fool anyone that love was in the air between the Principal and the Homeliving Specialist. I continued to repeat a favorite saying that I'd assumed since coming to Kinlichee: *If I live for a thousand years, these will be my finest hours.*

53. Life Began Again

In May, amidst the blooming flowers and tomato plants we'd planted with the children of Kinlichee, and with the blooming of a new love, AC's mother came to visit her at our school. Although I had briefly met her back in November on a visit to the school, this time was different. She attended our sports awards banquet in the cafeteria where I was making speeches and giving out trophies. Mother Florine must have sensed something in her daughter because she remarked afterwards, "I really like Vincent; what a special man he seems to be." AC gave her an account of what was taking place.

I was black and AC was white. I wanted no problems, and I decided that the relationship would go no farther unless I had her mother's full approval. Although AC was forty and I was nearly sixty, I needed to have Mom's permission. While watering the tomato plants at the dorm one evening, Florine came along and I had the opportunity to talk with her. "I want to know if there are any reservations about my going with your daughter. Can you accept me having a relationship with her? Because, if you have any problem at all, I will end it right here because I don't want to cause difficulties for myself or for her."

I gave that speech and then Florine, with her gift for words, assured me that she was thrilled to hear the good news about our love. She talked about her daughter, and some of the misadventures she'd encountered, and how it seemed that she now had the opportunity to have a happy life with a good person.

We kept our relationship secret at the school because of the government rules on nepotism. AC continued to address me as "Mr. Beach" and we were circumspect in our comings and goings. It's doubtful we fooled anyone, especially Johanna, the secretary. She gave a glowing, and knowing smile when looking at the two of us.

Lal and Sanjay drove up to Kinlichee to visit and I introduced AC as a friend. Kris had already met her on one of his visits to Kinlichee. Jenny, AC's only child, came to visit from Bluff, Utah. Jenny accepted me right away and seemed comfortable with the idea of her mother and me falling in love. My sons were a different thing; acceptance was a long ways off, but the introduction that Dad had a new friend was made.

While Florine was visiting that May, we thought it would be nice to go to Mass together on a Saturday evening. There was one problem: we shouldn't be seen together at the Catholic Church in Ganado where we would be well-known. We drove twenty-five miles to the isolated community of Klagetoh, near Wide Ruins Boarding School. There was a feeling of great peace when the three of us entered the ancient, hand-cut stone building of St. Anne's Catholic Church. After Mass, the warm and friendly Sister Maria Santo met us and said she thought we must be musicians.

"Do you play piano?" she questioned AC.

"No, not really, and never in public!" was AC's alarmed reply. I allowed that I played flute. Sister Maria wouldn't take no for an answer. The following Saturday night found AC and me at St. Anne's for Mass; her fingers dancing somewhere above the keys on the old electric organ, and me carrying the Mass music on my silver flute.

We bought a small electric organ and kept it at the White House so that AC could get in shape. Soon her confidence began to build, and our duo was acceptable as we played for the small Navajo congregation, Father Carroll, Sister Maria, and the elderly Sister Adrienne. We were folded into their love and care. AC, having had no church home for many years, made the decision to become a Catholic. With her already solid Christian faith, Fr. Carroll confirmed her in a special evening Mass on December 26, 1984. Jenny and I stood by her, laying hands on her shoulders. Sister Donna, from Page, Arizona, played the guitar. In that one moment it seemed that all the sad and bad things that had happened to both of us were forgiven and put to rest. We were stepping out into a new life of faith and hope. It was exciting, and the line from my favorite song seemed so appropriate: *And life began again the day you took my hand.*

54. A New Home

East met West at Thanksgiving 1984. I took AC, her mother Florine who had come to visit from Vancouver, Washington, and Jenny to Chandler and got them a room at Williams Air Force Base. We planned a more definite introduction that would include both our families. Kris took one look at Jenny, and laughing, said, "Are you really this pretty?" Hitting it off from the start, they were off for a round of fun over the next couple of days.

Lal was home from the University of Arizona, and Sanjay was home from Colorado State University. We imagined it would be a great time to become better acquainted, and cross some of the hurdles of blending a new love with our grown children.

It turned into a pretty emotional weekend when we encountered Miriam whom I hadn't seen for more than a year-and-a-half. I introduced her to AC and Florine thinking that at least she might like to meet them. I talked the situation over with the boys and decided that we should invite their mom to our usual Thanksgiving dinner at the

213

base dining room. She accepted, and even prayed for the meal and the family.

Afterwards, linking arms with AC and asking to take a walk with her, Miriam implored that she leave Vincent alone and give her a chance to get him back. AC assured Miriam that whatever Vincent wanted to do would be accepted. Over the weekend, there were more meetings and regrets expressed. I was taken by surprise because I thought that Miriam was glad to have me out of her life – I'd never heard otherwise until that weekend.

There was no turning back the clock. The divorce was final and I was relieved because I felt that Miriam and I had no chance for a harmonious life together. Whatever had been in the past, whatever mistakes, missteps, or unwise decisions that might have been made, there was no way to change what had taken place. I wanted a fresh start and a chance to live a peaceful life. I hoped our families could come together and accept each other.

Quietly, secretly, Monday, January 14, 1985, AC drove her 1978 Chevy van and I drove the government vehicle to Chinle. Justice of the Peace Glenn E. Stoner married us in the presence of two Navajo witnesses. We signed the paperwork, stopped by a donut shop, and returned to work. AC wore the wedding ring set we'd gotten on layaway at the base. We needed to keep our marriage a secret otherwise one of us would likely have to leave Kinlichee and work elsewhere. So we continued to live across the street from each other. It wasn't terrible, but we felt badly not to tell our kids or AC's mom. We consoled ourselves that, in time, they would understand that we wanted to be together. (Later we received the Sacrament of Marriage in the Catholic Church by our favorite priest, Fr. Gregory Nowel.)

I knew that we must prepare for the likelihood that I might have to retire, or *want* to retire. The school board was increasingly difficult to deal with. They went over my head to hire a special education teacher whose sister was a friend of one of the school board members. *Mr. Beach, why don't you want to help out one of your own (black) people?* I lost the bitter controversy and was forced to hire "Miss Pickens" from Texas, an elderly lady, who seemed as if she'd never been in a classroom. The handwriting was on the wall: I would not be able to have much control in directing the school.

AC and I made the trip to Chandler to buy a house and get prepared for the possibility of a move. Kris and Ruth were living in the motor home in the parking lot of the Delphi Business College in Mesa. Ruth, a lovely young woman of nineteen, was pregnant. The motor home had caught fire and was nearly unlivable. It seemed hardship upon hardship was being visited upon them. We wanted to buy a house so that they could have a place to live, and we would have some security.

Two days into the search, first with a realtor that proved to be unhelpful, then on our own, we walked into the house at 603 East Carla Vista Drive, Chandler, Arizona, and felt at home. It was empty and quiet; a red rose bush in the back-yard, and a Japanese plum tree out front. It looked like the perfect place. I secured the veteran's home loan, and with no down payment, the house was ours in twelve days. With Kris and Ruth joyfully helping, we moved in. Such a feeling of relief! They had the back bedroom, we had the master bedroom, and there was one small bedroom still empty. I planted grape vines, a fig tree, and began to turn 603 into our oasis.

55. Around the Table

During this time, Lal gradually lost his scholarships at the University of Arizona. Trying to pay for his schooling and dorm was beginning to be a financial strain for me, and I encouraged him to come home, live with his mother, and go to Arizona State University. He decided to make the change, but my enthusiastic and industrious student was losing his way. The trauma of death and divorce had definitely affected him. His older brother Jaswan died of Lupus which Lal had suffered with for several years. Although no research supports any transference of Lupus between two people, it seemed to Lal that somehow Jaswan got the disease and died.

Within a short time of living with his mother, there was a blow-up and Lal moved into the extra bedroom in our new home. That seemed like the perfect arrangement. But Lal was increasingly depressed. When I came down for the weekends, we would have long hours of talking around the kitchen table. He wanted to abandon his medication and "if death came, so be it." His probing question was, "What is to be gained by a few extra months of life?"

I repeated the most important words of counsel that I knew; *Life, even with the pain that you suffer, is preferable to death. You are not just living for yourself, but for the people who love and care for you.*

My humorous and vibrant young son was sinking into despair. The steroid drug Prednisone, used to treat Lupus, can cause severe mood-swings and depression of which we were not aware. He fought with Kris and I got the dreaded phone call that Lal had been arrested for domestic violence when he broke things and threatened Kris. With that arrest, he had a record on top of his other problems. My heart sank as I wondered what would be the outcome of that episode.

He went back to his mom's to live for a short time and then moved to an apartment with his best friend John De Lught. He seemed to take on a little hope in life. Money ran out and he came back to live at our house. We were still coming home on every other weekend from the reservation and, although there were anxious moments, life seemed to be settling down.

Lal dropped out of college and took a job as a telemarketer. He did quite a good job as "Pete Simpson" working for King Tool Company selling tools over the phone. He once again shared funny stories about his work, but there wasn't enough money in such a job. He tried to join the Army and the other services. On the questionnaires he was asked about pre-existing medical conditions and he couldn't lie – he was turned down. He applied at the police department, but was turned down because he had been arrested for domestic violence.

Lal had a beautiful young girlfriend named Michelle. She couldn't understand his depression, and yet was about the only one who could make him smile. Looking back, we were all glad that he experienced the highs of first-love. I was pleased that he seemed to take to heart the old adage *as long as there is life, there is hope.* I could not accept the thought of a young man who self-destructed.

Telemarketing was taking a beating in Phoenix and it seemed Lal loved that kind of work. He and Michelle had broken-up, which was a stormy process, and he decided that he would move to Denver, Colorado, the city of his young boyhood.

56. New Life, New Work

Retirement looked good for 1986. Five months after our secret wedding, we were found out, and our Kinlichee staff proved to be happy for us. They threw their favorite kind of party – a potluck and we felt loved and accepted by our friends and co-workers. We even had a cake to cut. The downside was that Ft. Defiance Agency would not allow me to be her supervisor due to nepotism regulations. She resigned and went to work as a School Counselor for Ganado Middle School. It was a nice job for her, but I sure missed our daily working together.

I was almost sixty-two years old and I began to make calls to Washington, D.C. to find out what my financial situation would be if I retired. After much talking and checking, I discovered that my Air Force pension and civil service retirement would be put together and somehow I would come up with a comfortable monthly income – not a lot, but with some supplements, we could manage.

In June of 1986, with final farewells to my little school in the valley, we moved the last of our belongings to our home in Chandler. With the help of my sons, we'd already built a picket fence around the entire backyard. Ralph and Sylvia were right at home and soon pigeons, turtles, rabbits, and chickens joined our household. Our baby granddaughter Keasha, born July 5, 1985, would be part of our life everyday.

That summer of 1986 was lots of fun. We went swimming at the base pool, played ping-pong at the Recreation Center – still trying to beat Mr. Fuller, and we weren't strangers on the golf course. We worked at establishing a blended family in which all of the kids were adults. They needed the traditional home base that had been knocked out from under them. I sang "Tea for Two" and danced around the house with my first grandchild trying to put her to sleep (many times).

We worked at having family meals. Sometimes they were tense affairs and I had to counsel AC as she was losing patience. She felt she was invisible to the boys. At times she got pretty mad, but I helped her to remember that time would heal and not to go against my old dictum, *Sorrow is bourne in a hasty heart.* Most of the time, she listened to me.

We drove the old van up to Vancouver, Washington to attend AC's twenty-fifth high school reunion. That was kind of funny. Even though I was twenty years older than everyone there, most thought I was a peer. It was fun meeting her old friends and we vowed to return to the thirtieth, which we did. I've only missed one since that time.

I was retired, but I wanted to fulfill my dream to teach college students. I applied and was accepted to Rio Salado Community College and taught Psychology to my first class beginning August 1986, just two months after my civil service retirement. I was on my third career – age sixty-two – I was on "Cloud Nine". There was a lot of studying, reading student papers, and making notes to prepare for classes. Within a year, I was an adjunct faculty member for Chandler-Gilbert Community College on the brand new campus; night classes, day classes, teaching three courses per semester. I was called on to teach anything to do with Psychology, Political Science, or Arizona Government.

I had coaxed AC to apply for the part-time job of Catholic Religious Education Coordinator at Williams Air Force Base Chapel. She was scared because she knew so little about the Catholic traditions, but she knew about education. Fr. Vern Schueller hired her and she was thrilled to be involved in Christian work for the next seven years. Much of our life revolved around activities in the base chapel.

To supplement our income and keep in the mix of educational life, we both became substitute teachers for Chandler Schools. I mainly substituted for music and AC worked anywhere she was needed; those fun days continued for nearly seventeen years.

57. Is This It?

"Is this it?" was Kris's searching question while we were bar-
becuing in the back yard on a Sunday afternoon. It didn't
seem too exciting or fulfilling for a young man who still held
on to the dream of becoming a pro-golfer. He had a wife, a
baby, and another baby on the way. And I was thinking that
being a parent to adult kids may be even harder than all the
little kid stuff that had gone before.

I had cajoled, lectured, counseled, and finally kept silent
as I saw this young couple struggle. We sponsored Kris for
the Ben Hogan Mini-Tour and off he went leaving wife and
baby home. Ruth missed him and took the baby and flew to
meet him. He came back home midway through the tour.

About this time Kris, a pregnant Ruth, the baby Keasha,
and Lal were living with us. One night at dinner I very gin-
gerly approached the subject that it might be time for each
of the adult kids to pitch in ten dollars a week to help with
groceries and utilities. There was a stony silence. Kris, the
first to comment, stated, "Well, the handwriting's on the
wall. It's time to move out."

I had always promised my boys that they would have a home with me. I didn't want to feel guilty about asking for some help, but in light of the difficulties they had endured in growing up, I felt awful. There are probably many parents that share the same sentiment. There was no way to make up for my being gone so much or to get back what was lost from their childhood. I simply needed a few dollars to help with the expenses as I no longer had a big salary.

Kris moved his family out and we visited them in their new apartment down on Dobson. Ruth was working steadily as she always had. Kris was working on a regular job and running home to take naps. He loved his freedom. And he was still playing golf. Lal stayed on with us and paid the requested amount, although he didn't like to give it to me, but rather to AC: "Here, you can give this to Dad."

"Okay," she smiled. They had begun to be on much more friendly terms.

Kris and Ruth had gotten married suddenly one weekend before our permanent move to Chandler. We had received a phone call at Kinlichee; "I'm going to marry Ruth today before I change my mind," Kris said with a big laugh. We tried to be the kind of parents to adult children we thought appropriate. It was hard to stand by and not tell them what to do. Despite Kris's lack of enthusiasm, Ruth planned a big first anniversary party because she hadn't gotten to have a nice wedding. "I'll have it with or without him," she had declared. We weren't able to attend, but we learned the next morning that the young couple had a bad fight after the party and the police were called.

That precipitated divorce proceedings and my promising oldest son began to slip into the abyss of crime and courts. His brothers Lal and Sanjay and I sat around our kitchen table and had a conference with Kris. He was adamant that he knew what he was doing. But it seemed that the divorce, and loss of the everyday life with his children, had derailed him. All I could do at that point was pray for him and try to maintain our communication.

58. Dreams

Eric, my oldest brother, and his wife Janet were living in Milton Keynes, England. They were anxious to meet AC ("Anni" as most people called her) and to renew acquaintance with me. In 1987, we flew to Gatwick Airport, in London, and were met by Raymond, my nephew, and Eric. Wow! We stood looking at each other, thinking how much we each looked like Mas T, our father. My first words were, "How you doing, Old Man?"

My brother, who never lost his Jamaican lingo, replied, "Joos fine, Mon."

Missing from the welcome party was my irrepressible brother Kenneth who had been on his way to being a great drummer back in the forties. We hadn't kept in good touch over the years, but his German wife had sent a letter letting me know that he died of a brain tumor in Bristol during June, 1973. That made me sad.

For the next five days we reminisced and I got acquainted with my nephews: Raymond, the railroad man, and Kevan, the poet. Forty-five years had flown by since we were together in London; Eric and I making gigs and working to realize our dreams. "Why did we wait so long?" we kept asking each other. After a few jubilant days talking, singing Bill Wither's "Lean on Me," and promising to fly Janet and Eric to Arizona for a visit, we returned home.

I was somewhat bewildered by my brother. When I had been with him during the forties in England, he was full of dreams and plans. He put a beer in his glove compartment, and rode off to a gig feeling happy that he was playing music. Somewhere those dreams were put aside and he never found them again. He worked for the post office, retired, traveled nowhere and, as far as I could tell, had little interest in much except for his cars. He'd owned at least *eighty* old cars during his life.

I made up my mind that I would get him to America. He began to dream about that, and after several discussions and letters, we convinced Janet and him to fly (for the first time) and visit us in Arizona. We also traveled to Jamaica for a whirlwind four days and renewed our friendship with our sisters, Minnette and Mavis, and many family members. Eric and I prayed over the graves of our mother and father behind the house. The trip, although very expensive, was appreciated, and Eric and Janet returned to England rejuvenated.

Eric and Janet made one more trip to Arizona, and we made one more to England. We last saw Eric in 1998 before he was diagnosed with Parkinson's disease. He drove us around in his newest car and seemed at ease behind the wheel. The three of us made a journey by train and bus into London and I fulfilled my dream of finding Number One Blundell Street. I stood looking at the old brick building and felt, once more, the thrill of learning new tunes with my brothers and buddies more than fifty years prior.

Eric's chief joy was to listen to the radio and tinker with

his car out in the bungalow parking lot. Towards the end of his life, Janet sold his car and he no longer had even that to occupy his thoughts. His final years were spent going to a day-care facility, which he hated. He died in the hospital on April 1, 2003 of a total system failure.

I was reminded, through my brother's death, that no matter what limitations we might have, we must strive to live life to the fullest every day so that we arrive at our final destination with a sense of satisfaction. The lesson is taken to heart as I deal with a chronic disease in my own body. The River of Life is always before us: *Don't throw away your stick till you cross that river!* Never!

59. Go, My Son

One chilly November day in 1988, Lal packed up his little red Nissan pickup and headed for Denver. He had come over the night before for a big dinner and to hug his beloved niece and nephew, Keasha and Vance, and to play with them once more. I gave him some money, some last words of encouragement, and the words of a Navajo song ran through my mind, and later, I thought I should have sung it for him:

Go, my son, go and climb the ladder. Go, my son, go and earn your feather. Go, my son, go and make your people proud of you.

I watched him drive away and thought his move to Denver was a very *brave* thing to do. Although he didn't have a job, his brother Sanjay was there and so he left with some confidence. His collect phone calls were always welcome, and we chatted for long periods of time about his funny adventures. He found an apartment in someone's basement, and a job in telemarketing which was not too secure.

Lupus had been dormant for months and the doctor

thought it might be receding. Lal said he was feeling great; just worried about money. He'd had a wonderful Christmas with Sanjay's fiancée Kristy and her family. It was gratifying to know he was enjoying himself on his pioneering mission.

Sanjay and Kristy planned their wedding for February 4, 1989. AC and Jenny and I were invited. Miriam was also invited. Lal was to be the best man. Jenny flew in from Washington, D.C. where she was headquartered with the United States Marines Corps. Lal picked her up from the airport and they had hours of intense conversation. It was such a joy to watch the two of them; like long-lost brother and sister. Lal invited the three of us to stay in his basement apartment and we had a great time.

The wedding rehearsal was long and, I believe, during the coldest temperature Denver had experienced in one hundred years; minus fifteen degrees. We were cold! Lal drove us everywhere in our rental car and the four of us formed a special bond which had been absent in prior visits.

Sanjay and Kristy were a stunning couple. Sanjay, Lal and me in our shiny silver-black tuxedos (we called them our salamander suits), the bridesmaids in black velvet, and Kristy in her white wedding gown with the longest train I'd ever seen, caused everyone to sit up and take notice. Every tiny detail of the wedding was perfect.

The dinner and dance at the Doubletree Hotel was some of the most fun we'd ever had. Lal, as best man, made a brilliant toast and speech to the new couple. Miriam seemed to be having a great time and had a "seat of honor" with the bride's family. Lal remarked, "I can't believe it! There's my mother out there dancing up a storm. And look at Jenny dancing with everyone. They are usually the two wall-flowers." He was happy over that.

Sanjay said, while having a dance with AC, "I was afraid

this might be a tense day, but it's turned out to be really great."

Kris was the only person missing from that perfect family event. The story is yet to be told, but the probation officer wouldn't allow him to leave Arizona to travel to Colorado.

It was a joyful parting as Lal drove us to the airport. We had finally found acceptance and a caring from this son, and we knew it would be this way forever. How could anyone have guessed, or even imagined, that Lal's stay with us was coming to a close. He promised he'd come home for Christmas and we'd be together again.

60. Love you, Lal

Three days after our return from Denver, Lal called in jubilation. He said that the day we left he'd returned to his apartment and fallen down on his knees and prayed that he'd find a better paying job in something worthwhile. Within a couple of days, he had an interview and was hired at First Trust of Denver. He began his climb in the corporate world of securities and was enrolling in college to finish his degree. It seemed as if all our prayers were answered.

In June, he called to say that he'd found a much nicer apartment and that he loved his job and was making quite a hit at work. It seemed he had climbed the mountain of hardship and found new friends, a new outlook, and a renewal of his great spirit. His best friend, John De Lught, went up to Denver for a week-long visit in July. They could find things to laugh about when no one else saw the humor. They burned the midnight-oil running around town, even visiting the brewery for beer samples. The week ended and John returned to California where he was working in air traffic control.

It was a merciful God that reserved Lal's final week of activities to be savored with his best friend. But that week must have been taxing, both physically and emotionally. He was alone again and working hard. He made a call or two that he wasn't feeling so well and I urged him to get to the doctor right away.

On Friday, July 28th, Kristy, his sister-in-law, took him to the hospital. He called, and AC and I each talked to him, wished him well, and said to let us know if he needed anything. AC said, "Love you, Lal."

"Love you, too," he replied.

Kristy called on Saturday night July 29th, shaken, and said that I had better get up to Denver because Lal was really sick. She also called his mother to go.

Sanjay was in New York playing for the Jets in the National Football League, and Kristy was taking care of Lal at the hospital. I thought as I always did through the years; Lupus has raised its ugly head and needs to be put back in its bottle. Right after church on Sunday, July 30th, I caught a plane to Denver. Kristy met me at the airport and we went directly to the hospital.

I had never seen Lal look so sick. The doctors and nurses thought he had a recurrence of Lupus and that he would stabilize in a few days. The doctor said that he wasn't sure what was going on, but they intended to run some tests on Monday. Miriam had arrived earlier in the day and was ministering to him, along with Kristy and her mother Joyce. We made small talk and tried to cheer him up. Joyce got him some pudding and he made feeble attempts to eat. He drank some water and, for the next several hours, that was all he wanted.

At nine o'clock, the two mothers and Kristy said their goodnights and left. *How was I to know that this was his last night on earth? How was I to know that within a few brief hours he would be with his Maker?* I do know, however, that I was privileged to sit on the edge of his bed. Once in awhile he tried to make conversation, but it was unintelligible. I continued to try and encourage him through the night; one of the *roughest* nights I've had in my life.

He asked me to rub his legs because they were cold and he couldn't feel them. I spread another blanket over my son and tucked him in. I prayed once again, as I had only six years ago: *Lord, this is a bitter cup for one so young; if this is to be his lot, then Thy will be done. Into your hands, Almighty Father, I commend the soul of this Thy child and bring him to the full acceptance of your grace and blessing.*

I prayed for the mighty healing power of God to come down and touch and heal my boy. I must have prayed all night. And as the dawn came, I looked at Lal and it appeared that some improvement had occurred. The nurse brought in his breakfast, but he could not feed himself. I fed him; he opened his mouth and took the food, but appeared oblivious to what I was trying to do. His eyes seemed to be looking far away.

The doctor finally came in and said that it was time for them to run some tests and do a CT scan. The nurse and orderly placed him on a gurney and headed for the elevator. As he was wheeled by me, I squeezed his hand.

I took the next elevator to the ground floor, with the intention of going down the street to walk around for awhile and try to clear my head. I was just about to exit the hospital when the intercom blared, "Mr. Beach, report to the emergency room immediately." I was in the revolving door, so rather than break my stride, I continued the circle, and came back into the hospital.

I made a mad dash to the emergency room and found a team of doctors all rushing about and saying very little. I confronted one of them and demanded to know what was going on. He told me that Lal had gone into cardiac arrest and that they were trying to revive him. I remember finding a phone to call Kris, but as he wasn't home, I gave the message to Tammy, his girlfriend. For the next two hours, medical personnel were going in and out of that room with various types of equipment. Finally, the doctor I had spoken to earlier came to tell me: "We did everything we could, but without success. We've lost your son." He also stated that they would perform an autopsy to determine the cause of death. (The report showed that he died of a massive infection which can be a cause of death in Lupus.)

Miriam, who had returned to the hospital, collapsed crying and screaming in the hallway. I stood there trying to comprehend what the doctor was telling me. I went in to see Lal and he was lying there in the middle of the room. I touched him and he was cold.

I called once more to tell Kris but he wasn't there and I gave the saddest news to Tammy. She called AC who was just home from supervising Daily Vacation Bible School at the base chapel. She and four-year-old Keasha sat on the floor crying, AC told me later and wondered why I didn't call – I still don't know.

I spent that Monday night alone in Lal's apartment thinking and wondering how he could just die. I felt a sense of relief that he was now free of that dreadful disease – he was angry to be so young and so sick. Once again, he saw his dreams going down the drain. I found his wallet with a handwritten note giving his instructions on what to do with his belongings, *and* with the admonition for "no one to fight over anything." He must have known that the return of the illness, and its severity, could bring about his death.

I made the arrangements to fly home with his body following the completion of the autopsy. Miriam flew back earlier to Phoenix on a plane with Kristy, and waited for

Sanjay to arrive from New York. We were quiet and sub-
dued and just trying to get through the *monumental* thing
that had happened.

AC, at home, had made all the funeral arrangements so
that we could have a beautiful celebration of Lal's life. The
words of love, of sorrow, the sincere grief, the uncontrollable
emotion of Michelle his former girlfriend, Sanjay's tribute
to his fallen brother, and my few words, were all testimony
of the great love we felt for this young man.

After the service at Bueler's Funeral Home, we followed
the hearse to Queen of Heaven Catholic Cemetery. The casket was blessed by the priest, we sang "Amazing Grace," and
tried to console ourselves that Lal was at peace. His grave
lies beside his brother Jaswan's grave under the tall pine tree.
I rarely visit, but Sanjay does every time he comes home.

61. John 15

The summer of 1989 was searing hot in the Valley of the Sun. I was my usual practical self and showed little outward emotion following the passing of Lal. Florine, AC's mother, had hurried to Chandler to be with us for the services. We'd missed Kris's twenty-ninth birthday which had fallen on the first of August; the day after Lal had died. Kris, also stoic in the aftermath of his younger brother's death, requested to talk with Florine, his step-grandmother, with whom he'd had other personal conversations.

Florine bought Kris a small maroon-colored tea kettle and we dropped her off at his apartment for the afternoon. He made her a cup of tea and the two settled down to talk. She never shared their conversation, but both seemed to benefit from the time alone.

I drew upon my deep feelings that life is *not* for us to control. We do not come with a contract about how long it will be. There are no answers to the *Why?* questions. I felt comforted in the knowledge that the Lord Almighty was in control of our comings and goings and that I must rest my faith in whom I believe to be the Creator and Sustainer of All Life.

I missed teaching only one class at the college. I didn't miss a Sunday of directing the Catholic Choir at Willie – what we affectionately called Williams Air Force Base. I tried to keep life as normal as possible. But I had a new awareness of the *love* of people around me. All of the Air Force chaplains from Willie had come for Lal's funeral. The new priest, Fr. John Vail, had led the service, not at the Catholic chapel, but at the funeral home. He had done a commendable homily on John 15 which we had requested. That reading on love deviated from the usual Catholic Mass for the Dead. Fr. Vail later remarked, "After seeing all of the people at the funeral and hearing their words, I understood why you chose that reading."

I felt comforted by all the expressions of sympathy in cards that came, even from Lal's place of work at First Trust. In his short time on the job, he had made a pleasant impact with his humor, character, and work ethics. During his life of twenty-four years, he had found peace and direction as a follower of Jesus. I had to accept what had happened with the assurance that he was Home.

"Vincent, I can't believe it, but I think I'm pregnant," said AC. Between our forty-five and sixty-five years, we had managed to create a life and we were filled with hope – a baby would be so welcome. I wanted to adhere to my philosophy to *only tell who has a need to know*. Although AC would be prone to tell the world, I thought it best, especially in light of what we had just been through, to keep this piece of news to ourselves.

For nearly four months Dr. Hamilton at the base hospital was the only one who knew. We asked that our news be kept confidential. AC had to rest at home as there were a few problems and her job at the chapel was kept going by others. We watched the little one on ultrasound, and thought the baby was *meant* to be.

We were sent downtown for counseling on late-age babies and to get an amniocentesis test. We were in anticipation of finding out if we would have a little boy or girl. The wand moved over her already-large abdomen and the baby looked perfectly formed. AC said, "I can't see the heart beating."

The technician replied, "It's not. I'll get the doctor." We looked at each other – the dream of a new little Beach had come to an end. We had to let go and get on with our lives, or we would have been overwhelmed by sadness – too much had happened too quickly.

We settled down to maintaining our home as a haven for our children and grandchildren. A sense of completion was found in them. Our marriage remained strong – we felt that we'd been brought together by *destiny* and we would complete whatever mission God required of us.

62. Wide Receiver

"Go Sanjay, go!" I heard the chants all around me. I was quiet for the most part, intently watching my kid as a wide receiver for the San Francisco 49ers, the Green Bay Packers, and again the 49ers, and finally the Denver Broncos. From 1988, upon his graduation from Colorado State University, he entered into a career in the NFL.

We took the newspapers from the teams and tried to learn the names of all the players. We tried to understand what was actually happening on the field and also behind the scenes. Sanjay sent for us to see several of his games and that was great. It was always a big thrill to meet him afterwards outside the locker room and see the people gather around to get his autograph and speak to him.

One Sunday, while he was playing with the Packers, we rushed off after church at the base chapel to get to the Stadium Club Sports Bar down on Chandler Boulevard. Not having cable television, we went there to see the games. We walked in just as Sanjay scored a touchdown on the huge TV screen and everyone was yelling and excited because he was a hometown boy. No one knew who we were and we quietly went to a booth and said nothing. That was one of our best memories of the NFL years.

He was known as a journeyman player, popular with players and coaches, and he was steadfast in his commitment to living a Christian life at all times. Coaches like George Siefert and Mike Holmgren knew that he could be counted on to give his best on and off the field. He played with some of the greatest players in the NFL during the nineties: Joe Montana, Steve Young, Jerry Rice, John Taylor, Brett Favre, Sterling Sharpe, Reggie White, and John Elway.

Kristy was a "rock" for her young football player. I remember being in San Francisco for a game and the team went to a hotel to stay together the night before the home game. Sanjay called and I heard Kristy praying for him on the phone – a heart-felt prayer for encouragement and safety. She made friends with many of the wives and carried her role as a player's wife with dignity and humility.

In Green Bay, Kristy gave birth to their first baby, Kalpana – a Hindu word for "creation", and they were joyful. Grandma Florine, during a visit when we all gathered in Chandler, couldn't get over how a great big football player could change a little baby's diaper so skillfully and with such tenderness. That's how he was: he participated in every aspect of life with his family.

Doors were open to Sanjay to be a witness for his Christian faith. He worked with Fred, a former teammate, to mentor teens. He gave motivational talks at schools. He always was open about his faith in Jesus. He eventually became a board member for the Lupus Foundation in Colorado, as well as a financial supporter.

Knowing that football wouldn't go on forever, Sanjay began to take classes trying to decide what he would do for his next career. Studying and interning with Smith Barney

Financial in Green Bay, he eventually became a Financial Advisor and started his climb up the corporate ladder and into the realm of management. After nearly three years of hard work, Sanjay earned an MBA degree from Colorado State University in May 2006 and we traveled to Colorado for his graduation.

Sanjay and Kristy manage to run a tight ship with their four children; everyone involved in sports, church, mission trips, school activities – they somehow do it all. It's great to see a young couple work together to build a loving and productive family.

63. Strings

Poking around in Brindley's music store, which is now a 99-cents shop on Galveston Street, I looked at the polished, chestnut-colored cello and thought about how I'd always wanted to play one. I was strictly a horn man even now playing the flute at church and directing the choir. But I longed to try and learn that beautiful, mellow, orchestral instrument. AC, in her often-impulsive manner, said, "Get it. Why wait? If you study cello, I'll try and learn to play the mandolin." I plunked down six-hundred dollars and went home with my new cello and a couple of books.

Well, I found out why I was a horn man. The cello was hard, but I was determined to play. That was January, 1992, and I was sawing away and not making much progress. I was also teaching Keasha, my first grandchild, to play the flute. In spite of my cello troubles, we gave our first home concert to a captive family audience on Thanksgiving. Grandma Anni accompanied us on the piano, and we were all smiles.

I wasn't able to progress on my own, but I sure hated

to have to pay a teacher. It just wasn't in my nature. For the most part I'd taught myself or relied on friends to learn the other instruments. AC insisted that, for both our sakes, I find a teacher.

Debra Pearson, cellist for the Arizona Opera Company and a "teacher wonder" agreed to work with me, and I studied with her for two years. The book, *Never Too Late* by John Holt, his story of taking up the cello after age fifty, was an inspiration to me. I worked hard and was able to crank out some songs and AC and I had lots of fun playing duets and sometimes trios with Keasha. I taught two other grandchildren, Vance and Micsha, some cello. I think they decided the instrument was too heavy to pack around, but they did sound pretty good playing in the school orchestra.

In the meantime, AC became a mandolin fanatic, tried to teach herself, found a teacher, and eventually made her debut into bluegrass. Bluegrass was about the farthest thing from my mind in the world of music. But I helped her get the Jam Pak Blues 'N' Grass Neighborhood Band going beginning in 1994. Mostly I helped her make canjos; the single-string stick and can beginning instrument. Even that seemed somewhat hard to play.

Our whole life became wrapped up in music; kids and instruments all over the house and weekly rehearsals for which I am the *Supreme Bologna Sandwich Maker*. Though, at times, the whole project has seemed overwhelming, I have given my support to my partner because it makes her happy and I believe in what she's doing.

I got a viola, toyed with the string bass, practiced violin – begging lessons from Jam Pak kids, took guitar lessons, and now I'm trying to play the banjo. We don't play jazz or the great standards because we have to stick to traditional bluegrass. But I have lots of fun playing and singing with Jam Pak, and I'm presently the most senior member of the band.

64. Tattoo

B *ase Closure!* For most of us who geared our life around Williams Air Force Base at the east end of Chandler Boulevard (also known as Williams Field Road), that was a dirty word. We'd bridle when it was mentioned. "How could such a perfect pilot training base be closed? Look at all the new construction going on." A long list of possibilities for closing military bases around the world came out of Washington, D.C., but "Willie *couldn't* be one of them," we all said.

On March 31, 1993, I was standing in a ceremony on Willie's golf course, receiving a trophy (a treasured memento from those years) for being on the winning foursome of the Tattoo Golf Tournament. It was a thrilling moment. I had been paired with Colonel Robert Gatliff from another base and a couple of other guys who were crack players; we played the scramble to perfection. But the word "Tattoo" meant closure activities for the base; all the final events.

No more being the director of the Catholic chapel choir, no more cantatas that I loved to sing in, no more many activities to support with AC being the Religious Education Coordinator, no more being a member and president of the parish council, and no more social life with our many Air Force friends and chapel personnel. Since 1977 my family had utilized the base and all the retiree privileges I'd come to rely on; the commissary, BX, doctors, (I'd finally consented to a physical by this time) the NCO Club for a dinner out, and the golf course. Our tree on the ninth hole – my sons' initials were still carved deep into the flesh of the giant eucalyptus – that tree served as a kind of shrine for me. Our last Mass, with what was left of the choir, was May 16, 1993. I drove the old '78 Chevy van off the base for the last time, and we began a life without Willie.

I didn't want to attend Mass and not be part of the music. The few of us who were left decided we'd try and find a place to play. One church was too big – another seemed uninviting. On a Saturday night two weeks after the base closed, Linda Mennen attended Mass at Our Lady of Guadalupe in Queen Creek, a little country town south of Willie. She talked to the priest and we were playing Mass the following Saturday night; Steve Mennen on guitar, me on the flute, AC on mandolin, David Maestas on guitar and bass, and Lupe Angulo and Linda were our singers. We were soon joined by Juanita Brooks (who has loved me like a brother and throws me a birthday party every year).

The long-time Sunday morning choir got angry when Father Henry asked *us* to play for the Easter Vigil Mass in 1994 – we'd been there only ten months. Without notice, they quit! We stood talking out in the church parking lot and Steve said, "We can't let Easter happen without any music." So we came back and played the next morning to an enthusiastic congregation, and kept right on playing, adding faithful members along the way; every single Sunday for *thirteen years* and still going strong.

The choir was at an Epiphany party over at Mennen's and we wanted to have a jam. "On Eagle's Wings" is probably one of the most beautiful songs ever written, but it's *not* party music. We decided to make ourselves into a band; singing and playing a whole lot of Beatles, The Doors, The Eagles, John Denver and other popular stuff from the seventies and eighties – everything but jazz. Linda suggested calling us The Sparrow Band (David called us The Cracker Birds when we didn't sound good) and our theme song was "God's Eye is on the Sparrow" composed by Bob Hurd. Our drummer was Eugene Ball, another Air Force retiree buddy, and we were hot stuff. Busy lives have stood in the way of practicing and performing very much, but we've had lots of fun over the years playing music for parties. My sax and I can still play a nice break on "As Tears Go By." *It is the evening of the day; I stand and watch the children play...*

Within eight months, the Willie golf course was called Toka Stix: it was up and running under the management of the Gila River Indian Tribe, with help from a Texas golf course corporation. The green fee seemed exorbitant, but I still teed off every Tuesday with Frank, Charlie, Jim and the others with whom I'd played for years. Charlie Davis, although I hadn't known him well, gave me his number when the base closed. I called and we became playing partners nearly every Friday – searching out various golf courses that we could afford and hoping to find the elusive birdie.

65. La Forza del Destino

Don't throw away your stick till you cross the river was the often-repeated adage of my mother Miss Rosa and I repeated it frequently. My son Kris, handsome at six-foot-two, slim, dark complexion with curly black hair, and in his twenties, was throwing his stick as *far* as he could while in the middle of a raging river.

When his marriage with Ruth ended in divorce, (a very messy one complete with them punching each other while the mediator left the room during the court-ordered counseling) Kris became so full of anger that I didn't even know how to talk with him. He later said that when the most important things are taken from you, risk doesn't matter – caring about anyone, no longer a guiding force. He threw castigations my way and I tried to resist the temptation to argue or justify myself.

In January of 1988, following months of court and anger and aggression, he picked up little Keasha and eight-month-old Vance and tore out of town in his classy Mitsubishi. No words of counsel could stop him. I didn't know where he was. Just imagine how I felt when I saw posters in the windows of stores nearby: *Please help me find my children* with photos of Kris and my grandchildren.

I was truly disgusted with the path he had chosen. He could have seen the children, but he later said, "I know, but I wanted to hurt Ruth and that's the one thing I knew would hurt her." Within a few months his little holiday in Midwest City, Oklahoma, where he had graduated from high school, came to an end and he was extradited back to jail in Phoenix. The children were flown home safe and sound and we eventually had a reunion with them.

Kris was fortunate to only serve thirty days in jail for custodial interference. He went to work at Thunderbird Golf Course. But that wasn't the end: he had three beautiful options for his life work – golfer, teacher, or even a military career. Those were *my* choices for him, but only the one in golf held any appeal. No, he decided to study "street life" and in the midst of the years of the drug trade, he joined in and apparently was very successful. He began to extol the cleverness of "street people" and to move in the circles of dealers.

That made no sense to me whatsoever. He didn't know anything about street life, although according to him, he was learning fast. But he was vulnerable, and I was afraid he might get killed (he nearly was). The one thing that maintained during those frightening times was the fact that we never lost communication. He would tell us lots of scary stories. His brothers and I would counsel and try to tell him of the pitfalls. In the end, all we could do was pray that he would somehow be safe.

One night, while with his girlfriend Tammy, at his house on Butler Street in Chandler, the police staged a raid. It was awful to hear in the retelling. Only a trace amount of cocaine was found, but Kris was hauled off to jail and booked on charges of possession with intent to sell. *Oh God, no, not this!* I saw the worst happening – my kid, so full of promise, might face years in prison.

I got a thousand dollars from his bank account and went down to Madison Street Jail and bailed him out. Everything that occurred from there on out was *so* foreign to me that I just had to go on a wing and a prayer. He was eventually sentenced, and spent several months at The Towers jail on Durango Street awaiting prison. We visited him in the courtyard there. He wrote letters and sent his original cartoons to us. One day I took Keasha to visit him and, as I was carrying her out in my arms, she reached back and her finger got caught in the electronically-controlled door. She was crying and the jailer had to release her finger. I took her to an emergency room and her finger was just bruised. I was grateful, but all I could do was shake my head and think: *this is all so unnecessary.*

As I watched him being taken off to prison, I tried to maintain hope. He only spent a week at Ft. Grant but there he met more "street smart people" and later he loved to tell their stories. I just couldn't believe it and yet I knew, as his father, *my* job was to try and understand and be of help where I could.

He was to appear before Judge Ronald Reinstein, who is still a judge in the Maricopa County judicial system. I wrote a letter pleading for a second chance for Kris, detailing what I believed was his derailment following the divorce. I hand-delivered it to his clerk, went into the court with AC, and watched Kris be led in and stand before the bench. The judge glanced at me when he came into the court. He acknowledged the letter and my request that I would be responsible for Kris. He gave Kris a good talk and let him go with probation. *That* was the end of the drug dealing and life of crime.

Kris began to search for the stick. He took roads *I'd* never considered. He kept me abreast of all his dealings. He bought a townhouse down on 48th and Broadway. Over the next few years, he found his work and began dealing in real estate. He became president of the homeowner's association. He developed his renovation and maintenance skills, following somewhat in the things he loved to do as a boy. He was *greatly* admired in the area for his college education and his ability to lead, direct, boss and get things done. A whole section of townhouses which had been crime-ridden and dangerous began to turn around. He was and *is* a friend to many kids and adults who've been left wanting at life's table. He continues to deal in real estate all on his own, cares for his children, and is looking forward to the Senior PGA. I've grown very proud of him and the work he's accomplished and the man he has become.

His personal life has been *anything* but traditional. He never married again, but several more children have been born – beginning in 1992 with Ebony. With his children, and their mothers, have come other little people who also call me Grandpa. My extended family is large and I am grateful for each one.

La Forza del Destino – The Force of Destiny. What more can I say?

66. My Golden Years
or This IS It!

A trait that perhaps distinguishes me from the more aggressive "Type A" personality is my ability to be at ease in the routine of everyday life. I do not chafe at the ordinariness of the need to cook, eat, feed the animals, wash dishes, repair the cars – all the daily chores that keep a household and life running smoothly. I would do any task at hand. AC, who is a person that often operates on impulse – following her heart instead of her head, looks to me for the *steady presence* to help her creative energy be productive. Maybe that's one reason we've had such a harmonious relationship for over twenty years – and a whole lot of fun

My seventieth birthday present was a big surprise for me. Sanjay and Kristy came home and, under my very nose, everyone was scurrying around and wouldn't let me know what was going on. I could not contain my laughter when, in our living room, they produced the play AC had written titled: *Some of Your Life, Vincent Beach*. Everyone had roles

261

to play and the costumes were hilarious. And *my* two sons; I couldn't believe their act playing me at various times of my life. The video still causes us to laugh like crazy when we watch it every few years.

We made our last trip to England in 1998 for my nephew Raymond's wedding. AC and I took Eric and scouted out London until we finally located Number One Blundell Street. The memories of that first house, which I owned over fifty years ago, were still fresh. We celebrated with fish and chips at an African-owned joint, enjoying each other's company and quiet talk, and savoring what was to be our final journey in my brother's company.

That was the only "Space A" (free) trip, a benefit of my Air Force retiree status, which we've been able to take. England, Germany, and several nights on the gym floor at Mildenhall Air Force Base in England because there was "no room at the inn" (due to a major air show) was strenuous, but we had a blast. We played our flute and mandolin, ate great food, and enjoyed meeting new people.

However, a call home made us anxious to catch a flight although we still had to be patient a few more days. Colton Tiger Beach was born seven weeks early and Kris and Erin were parenting the little three-and-a-half pound baby at the hospital. We finally touched down, took the shuttle home, and got to the hospital to hold him. He appeared perfect. We took Erin and the baby home to her apartment two days later.

Keeping our promise that we'd do whatever we could to help, we took Nicholas, Erin's three year old son, home to stay with us for a few days so that his mom could recover from her C-section. During that time, I received a "Dear John" letter from Chandler-Gilbert Community College. *Mr. Beach, we have decided to go another direction for the Political Science department (I was the one and only adjunct professor for the subject) and we will no longer need your services.* That was that. No personal meeting, no reasons, no gold watch and chain for the thirteen years I spent doing a lot of teaching for the school.

Although I felt disappointed, it also seemed like the time was right. AC and I helped to care for Nick and Colton during the first year of Colton's life. It was somewhat remarkable to have daily responsibility for a tiny baby. He grew and flourished. His first genuine belly-laugh was looking at my face while I was holding and talking to him.

I kept my old cars running. The 1978 van that AC brought with her to our marriage had its fourth engine installed. The 1984 yellow Cadillac Coupe Deville was a beauty, but always needed help. And then AC, following a trip to California in the Weiland's motor home with twenty Jam Pak kids, decided we had to have a motor home.

There were always problems in transporting the Jam Pak Blues 'N' Grass Neighborhood Band to gigs. Down on Pecos Road, the perfect solution was parked there for sale: a 1972 motor home, looking like an ice cream truck, but with a big Ford engine. AC wanted it and, against my better judgment and expounding on my well-worn adage *Sorrow is bourne in a hasty heart,* I let her talk me into it. We actually paid the Mexican man, named Candy, seventeen-hundred dollars instead of the fifteen-hundred we had agreed on because AC felt sorry for him.

A whole book could be written about the adventures with that motor home and all the little kids. But AC was at her height of glory at the wheel with all the gear, the instruments, the young musicians packed in like sardines, and going down the road. Only one problem: the poor old motor home rarely made it anywhere without a breakdown.

Lots of money, ingenuity, and just plain luck were put into that twenty-four-foot, obsolete-brand *Bandwagon.* On one memorable occasion, after a week in the repair shop for overheating problems, we were loaded and heading to Prescott. No sooner had we started up that steep, long stretch of road by Black Canyon, than it quit, right there, and up against the guardrail. The only door couldn't open and the kids had to climb out the window and head up the hill away from danger. Fortunately, parents came back and took the kids on to Prescott for the bluegrass jam. The show had to go on!

We called for help (this was before we got AAA) and none came. I finally got out in the June heat and began to fiddle around. The wire harness was all burned. I don't know what I did, but after about an hour, it started. I told AC to move over, I got into the driver's seat just as a highway patrol pulled up, and I said, "We gotta go!" I made a U-turn and went *hell bent for leather* all the way home. AC called me "The Miracle Worker" after *that* close call.

After many more surgeries on that old wagon, many more breakdowns, and lots more money, we bought a 1988 Winnebago, and the band plays on.

67. Son-in-Love

She called me her son-in-love. My mother-in-law, who could speak with authority on almost any subject – a social activist (well ahead of her time), and a subscriber of "The Washington Spectator" – at age ninety-three came to live with us. Florine, following a series of compression fractures in her spine, and numerous trips by AC and her sisters to care for her in Vancouver, Washington, made the decision to move.

A temporary caregiver stuck a finger in Florine's soup to test the warmth, and my little mother-in-law was on the phone in a jiffy. "Is the invitation still open to come and live with you?" she asked. We gave her our master bedroom and bathroom and fixed it up nicely: an electric bed, her lift-chair, as much of her stuff as could be squeezed into the small space and the rest spilled over into the house.

From April 14, 2001 until her death on February 8, 2003, we both took care of her. She carried on her life as best she could: walking around our long block every day with her walker (often in the pre-dawn hours as she wanted to get an early start on her day), eating well, and keeping up her contacts with family and friends. She continued to write letters on social issues to her newspaper, *The Columbian*, in Vancouver. She practiced on her golden concert harp almost daily, and left the legacy of a new harpist, Gieselle Tambe-Ebot, a young high school friend of ours.

I would be lying to say that this was an easy time. Our freedom was severely restricted as we couldn't leave her alone too long. She liked a routine schedule and we made sure she had nutritious meals three times a day. She could be demanding in her quiet and subtle way. But I was grateful that we were able to have her with us, as she had always been one of my biggest fans.

I joined AC and her sisters Nyle, Janette, Miriam and niece Kathy around Florine's bed as we prayed and sang for her on her final journey following a stroke. I was privileged to hold her hand. She had always loved my large hands and I'm confident she *knew* it was me, right by her side. I stayed in her room alone when the guys came to transport her body to the funeral home, wanting to make sure she was taken care of properly.

We decided that she couldn't be returned to Vancouver without a celebration with her friends and family in Chandler. She was the Jam Pak Grandma, so the next evening we had a big bluegrass jam at the funeral home. We sang and played songs like "I'll Fly Away," "Flowers for Mama," and "Jesus, Make a Way for Mother," the song written especially for her by Mark Hickler, our banjo teacher. There was no casket so she was accessible to us all. The children messed with her hair and we all admired her angelic smile.

Then we were off to Vancouver for a gathering of the DuFresne families and all the final events. I served as a pallbearer with her grandsons, granddaughters, and great-grandsons, and set the cadence for our final walk. I felt a deep sense of appreciation for her life well-lived. We all helped "tuck her in" – the words of her grandson Peter – not leaving on that cold day of February 15th until all the sod was back in place.

68. Grandpa's Asleep

Back in Chandler, we rattled around in our house. Florine was missed, but we tried to pick up our old routines. We still worked out at the fitness club. I substituted in the schools, but it seemed like I *just* couldn't keep my eyes open. One day I got lost trying to find one of my school assignments on a traveling music job, and I just went home. I didn't even call anyone.

We took Jam Pak on a camping trip to Picacho, Arizona and AC drove the motor home and I drove the old '78 van. The motor blew just as I left the freeway. That was to be my last long-distance drive. Thanks to AAA, I got it towed all the way home and Bobby Robertson, our "Jam Pak Dad-Mechanic" set about to install engine number *five*.

AC traveled once more to Vancouver to attend a memorial for our mother at the Ft. Vancouver Seafarer's Center, another legacy of Florine's. I was alone for the weekend. Bobby was to come on that Saturday morning to work on the van to prepare for the new engine. He was late and I was trying to fool around with some of the parts. When he came at noon, I felt very tired, so I rested in the carport on the couch. I remember *nothing* after that.

Late in the afternoon, Kris drove by with the little kids and tried to pick up our Kizzee grandchildren, who lived close by, to take them swimming. He stopped at our house first, and honked, but no one came. He saw the door open and thought I must be out back. He drove on down the block to get the children, but they couldn't go. So he came by our house once more and honked. He said he wasn't even going to stop but then decided to send Colton to see if he could find his Grandpa. Colton came back to the truck and reported, "Grandpa's asleep in the chair."

It was a very hot day for May 10, 2003. Kris tried to rouse me. I told him that AC was in the backyard. He tried to help me stand, but I couldn't get up. Kris was really scared and called Sanjay in Denver to see what to do. Sanjay told him to call 911 right away. The paramedics came and did all their stuff and took me to the emergency room at Chandler Regional Hospital.

And then I was left to sit in the emergency room. Kris went to see to the children and to get help from Erin, their mother. Sanjay called the emergency room and demanded that they take care of me immediately and not listen to my comments, "I'm okay." My temperature was up to one-hundred-three degrees, blood pressure very high, and I was in *pain*.

AC called to tell me her plane had landed and she'd be home on the shuttle in a little while. Erin answered the phone at our home and said, "Did anyone call you about Vincent?" AC got the driver to get her to the hospital quickly and she took charge. It was a very scary night for my family, but I don't remember anything past Bobby coming to fix the van.

After all the tests and temporary treatments, it appeared

I had a huge infection, and I was admitted. AC and Kris stayed most of the night with me. Kris had run home and brought back a pillowcase with bananas, Pepsi and some cans of sardines along with my better slacks – "Just in case you want to go golfing!"

I was diagnosed with Strep A which had caused a massive septic blood infection. How it got there, no one knows. But the strong antibiotics began to do their work and I was actually released in a couple of days. I thought I would zip back into action and continue to work on the van.

That didn't happen. I began to have a lot of pain, bladder spasms, and blood in my urine. We went back and forth to the emergency room and urgent care. On top of all that, the antibiotics were making me sick. After several days, and with AC getting very mad, I was readmitted to the hospital. Under the care of a young guy, Dr. Shalipour, a team of specialists started to look at me. I had bladder cancer and what they called endocarditis (infection around my heart valves). From that time on, my life as I'd known it, changed.

Such illness was hard to accept or believe. I had walked eighteen holes of golf earlier in the week before I got sick. On May 9th, I had substituted at San Tan-Basha School in music although I realized I'd *slept* through most of the day. I had a cheerful talk with AC that Friday night about ten o'clock and knew she'd be home the following evening.

Now I was restricted at home on IV antibiotic drips three times a day, which AC was taught to do by a visiting nurse. I went each week to my new urologist Dr. Frank Simoncini for chemotherapy put directly into my bladder. I rested the whole summer, could walk only a short ways down the block, and AC was making me drink water. My diet became something like Florine's; lots of fruits and veggies, on time, and following guidelines for additional protein and stuff to fatten me up.

Through all the treatments and procedures, I did not have one bad side effect. I grew stronger and we returned to our choir duties at Queen Creek, Jam Pak resumed, I took longer walks, and we had lots of doctor appointments to make sure I continued to heal.

I realized later that the angels were watching over me or that Florine was busy directing traffic on that fateful day of May 10th. Kris said that he hadn't even planned to stop that second time because it was *so* hot and the kids were anxious to get to the pool. *We all knew that one of life's miracles had happened for me.*

69. Daughter and Friend

AC's sixtieth birthday was a double celebration, that November 15, 2003, of her life *and* my life. All of our families gathered. We had a huge festive party in our house and yard. A special marriage blessing for us was administered by Mark and Dianne Hickler on behalf of the Unification Church. We were all *so* thankful to play music, eat food from Soul 'N' the Hole, and laugh together once more. Jenny came home from Washington, D.C. for the event.

Jenny, my daughter by marriage, has always been close to me. Over the past twenty years, I have been so proud of her. A U.S. Marine for nine years, she also worked in various jobs while earning her BA degree from George Mason University in 1995.

She worked as a personal assistant to Marion Wright Edelman, one of the famous civil rights workers of the 1960s. She personally knew Medgar Evers' (a civil rights martyr) wife Myrlie, who was director of the National Association for the Advancement of Colored People (NAACP). She was moving in the circles of movers and shakers – this little girl who had been raised in *harsh* conditions on the Navajo Reservation.

I rubbed the boot of John Harvard for good luck in the courtyard at Harvard University in Cambridge, Massachusetts, and I was reminded of how far Jenny had traveled. I first met her when she was eighteen years old and at that time, she planned to become a beautician. We'd gone up to St. George, Utah to see her in beauty school. It had seemed, even then, that this new daughter of mine was *misplaced*.

I sat with her mother, on that warm morning of June 1999, among the educators of one of the most prestigious universities in the world and watched her receive a Master's Degree in Education. It was a time of elation. After three years of teaching in Washington, D.C. public schools, she has followed her dream to found a school with the mission to help change things for the boys of Ward Eight in Washington, D.C.

She's maintained her family ties with us even though she's the farthest away. She's paid for some of her nieces and nephews to visit her in D.C. And on July 23, 2003, she proudly accompanied her mother and me when we received a national award for *Excellency in Parenting* at the United States Capitol. (She had also come home in July 2002 when we were honored as Arizona Parents of the Year – an award based on our work with Jam Pak.)

We stayed in her new home, a 1920s brick row-house just north of the Anacostia River. We ate a delicious dinner gathered around her Grandma Florine's old mahogany dining table that she had inherited. I sat in the chair my father-in-law Ronald DuFresne had occupied for so many meals and thought of him. He had died before I was in their lives, but I liked to think he would be pleased for his daughter and granddaughter.

Jenny came home in July 2004 and remarked to her

mother that I was not the Vincent of former years. She suggested that I get to a neurologist and see what was going on. The voice therapist I had been seeing, and the ophthalmologist who was trying to check my vision, had already made similar suggestions. We kept thinking I was just taking a long time to recover from the endocarditis.

We got the appointment. The neurologist talked with me a long time, reviewed my history, asked me who the governor of Arizona was and I could only remember her first name "Janet". *Me, the political science instructor!* He sent me home with some pills and said, "If you're better with these pills, then it's likely you have Parkinson's disease."

Within four days, I cooked Kris's birthday dinner, participated in conversation, and seemed to walk with a little more bounce. And my eightieth birthday on September 25, 2004, was truly a time to celebrate: Parkinson's isn't life-threatening and I felt a little stronger.

Jenny wrote a letter to me for my birthday as she was not able to attend the party. I have included the entire letter in the book because it meant so much to me from this daughter *and* friend.

Dear Vincent,

The celebration of your 80th birthday is drifting into memory. I wanted to take an opportunity to acknowledge you and all that you have done for our family.

You came as a blessing to Mom. The tumultuous seas of life had tossed her about; the anchor she needed, the peace she needed, came through you. For this I am deeply humbled and grateful. It means more to me than you can ever know. My greatest joy is to see Mom happy, at ease, and joyful. I know that those qualities come from within her, but I believe that your steadfastness, patience, love, and support created the space for her to flourish; for her great spirit to come alive.

You are an amazing father! Your patience and wisdom have guided all your children and grandchildren to a deeper understanding of themselves and the lives we find ourselves creating. Your easy chuckle, great political conversation, and steady hand have always been something I've appreciated. I love the confidence you exude. Each of your children and grandchildren are better, more thoughtful people because of your contributions to our lives.

I often reflect on the life you and Mom have built for yourselves. Your relationship is one of the greatest love stories I have ever witnessed. On those occasions I'm home, I love to watch the dance the two of you have, the strength you each give one another, the kindness you each show one another, the joy you each bring to one another. These are attributes of your relationship I aspire to see reflected in mine. I attribute this beauty to the wisdom you have found through the journey of your life and your willingness to share this wisdom with your partner. I understand that the power of your relationship is found in the communication and respect you each bring to the other. I believe that you and Mom bring out the best in each other.

I am thankful to you for being part of my life. For showing me that great love is possible. For showing me that the past does not have to chart my future. I love you and all the many ways you have made my life better. Happy birthday! I look forward to seeing you soon.

Love,

Jenny

Thoughts of an Ordinary Man

My 1985 pristine Cadillac Fleetwood D'Elegance proved to be too large a temptation on January 2, 2005; sometime during that rainy night, it was stolen. (We had just been present at the birth of our first great grandchild.) I was still driving and I felt violated and quite isolated without my own set of wheels. A year later, Kris, having begun to restore the muscle cars of the fifties and sixties, readied a bright lime-green 1968 Chevy Impala. I bought it and drove the fifteen miles home. I loved old cars because I knew how to work on them. I was well into my neurological illness by this time, but I wasn't ready to give up on my driving.

Everyone was coming by and admiring my green Impala and talking about it, especially the kids. I was pretty proud and drove off to the Green Tree Dollar Store and it stalled in the parking lot. I couldn't get it started and there seemed to be no one who would help me. I went in the store and tried to call Kris and he didn't answer. I called AC several times and left messages but forgot to tell her where I was.

She found me after several hours and a lot of worry, and called AAA. The mechanic got the car started and I drove off without waiting for AC. I was lost immediately, going into oncoming traffic, then through a housing area, and finally onto Galveston Street – by that time surrounded by six Chandler police cars and a Gilbert fire marshal that had been following me from the dollar store and called in the report. I heard a blaring voice ordering me to pull over. Soon a fire truck and ambulance pulled up, lots of people from the low-cost apartments came out to watch, and AC finally drove up and jumped out to tell everyone that I had Parkinson's. The Chandler officers were very courteous, the paramedics checked me over and I was fine. I felt like it was all unreal and I was standing in a foreign place. I smiled and thanked everyone and the officers helped us get home.

I realized that in spite of seeing myself as "Disaster Plus," I was going to have to adjust. *If it's not dead don't throw it away*, that old adage from my mother Miss Rosa, reminded me that even if I couldn't drive, that I still had a lot of life left to live and I must not let myself go down.

As this family has moved from one place to another, welcomed new members by birth or association, and comforted those who've gone on, it seems that we have been blessed. We've looked disaster in the face and kept moving forward.

I don't believe we are here of our own making. I've always strived to abide beneath that enormous Power. We're *not* the big dog on top of the heap, but rather a member of the "whole" of creation. Some people think, "Beyond me, there's nobody." I think the opposite; because of this Power, I can adjust my thinking, allowing that there is *greater* than I. The timely words of Dr. E. Stanley Jones, a Christian writer and philosopher sum up what I think of God: "I don't know what the future holds, but I know Who holds the future." I am living these last years of my life with a condition called Progressive Supraneural Palsy; (not the Parkinson's as was first diagnosed) and over which I have very little control.

More important than ever is my mother's adage and the central theme of my memoirs: *Don't throw away your stick till you cross the river.* I can't give up for my own sake as well as for my partner (a guiding star in my universe), my family, and friends and fellow musicians, young and older. They expect me to carry on with my steadfast nature. I will do what I can to carry out my responsibilities to take care of myself and keep as healthy as I can. I'll try to be a peacemaker wherever I'm called. I won't complain about all the things I can no longer do. I'll plant a mango seed and wait for its green, shiny leaves to appear. I'll take a piece of bread to Webster, our gray goose, when she calls, and I'll take my walk and ride my exercise bike. I'll call my sons and the children and chat, knowing I'm still me and I have thoughts to offer and I can listen. I'll have AC drive me to get lottery tickets twice a week in hopes I might win something. I'll gladly let friends and family help me when I get turned around and can't find my way in my own house. I'm going to live and be part of daily life, our bands, our pets, our great and extended family.

I'm at peace in the world. I have no grudge, no particular hang-up with *anyone.* If each man shows peace to his fellow man, he will live in peace himself. And I pray *constantly.* I think without prayer, we'd be lost. Prayer is a constant source of strength; a crying out to a greater Power for help; a knocking at the door.

I'm an ordinary man. It is my hope and dream that you, who have read these pages, will have found something useful to enhance your journey in this life. I've always considered myself a private person and it's been with some hesitation that I've revealed my very personal experiences and reflections and those of my children. None of it was set down to hurt or castigate, especially my former wife. Through the experiences of others, we can all hopefully learn how to avoid the pitfalls that can make our lives and others unhappy.

Some of us sit and let opportunities pass right by which could help make a better life for ourselves and our families. Not *all* of us have an equal chance, but for each one there *are* opportunities. My word to you who follow is to seize an opportunity, however small, when it's presented. It may not come again. Seek out an ideal and believe in your abilities to reach your goals. Do *something* with your life that you can be proud of when it's all said and done. Your decisions early in life will have influence on the kind of life you make for yourself. Patience, constancy, hard work, and goals ever before you, will spur you on to make a worthwhile life – and love – let that small word be your power.

I sent my mother-in-law a little quote back in the 1980s and she kept it on her bulletin board as a reminder all through the years: *Dear Lord, fill my mouth with the right stuff and, Lord, nudge me when I've said enough.* I feel the nudge and it's time to bid you farewell for now. *The Book of Life is brief.* Each day counts. Not *one* should be wasted in senseless negativism or defeatism. Make it a joyous time. And remember: *Don't throw away your stick till you cross the river.*

May God bless you, and I'll keep you in my prayers.

Same as ever,

Vincent Collin Beach

Vincent Collin Beach (Son)

The Family Circle

Rather than a family tree, I prefer to think in terms of a family circle where sons, daughters, mothers, partners, and grandchildren are all included – regardless of formalities such as marriage or circumstances of birth.

Krishna Devi Beach – son
Jaswan Ali Beach – son
Lal Ramdin Beach – son
Sanjay Ragiv Beach – son
Jenny Frances DuFresne – daughter
Ruth Victoria Stamp – daughter-in-law
Kristine Raene Beach – daughter-in-law
Carla Ann Kizzee Williams – daughter-friend
Erin Conners – daughter-friend
Natalie Burton – daughter-friend
Keasha Marie Beach – granddaughter
Vance Christopher Beach – grandson
Ebony Lashay Kizzee – granddaughter
Colton Tiger Beach – grandson

Haley Mariah Beach – granddaughter
Nicholas Mark Conners – grandson
Micsha Diane Rae Carson – granddaughter
Hannah Victoria Carson – granddaughter
Eran Dupree Kizzee – grandson
Tyanna Katrice Kizzee – granddaughter
Tara Kathleen Kizzee – granddaughter
Kalpana Kristine Beach – granddaughter
Makis Lal Beach – grandson
Tariq Jaswan Alan Beach – grandson
Jalen Q Beach – grandson
Neomi Monet Beach – great-granddaughter
Vaughn Bailey – grandson-in-law

In February 2006, AC and I attended a healing Mass at Our Lady of Guadalupe Church in Queen Creek. Father O'Grady laid hands on me, and although I didn't get "slain in the Spirit" as did many around me, I felt a sense of peace. The very next day, AC met Miriam Cooderath, my former wife of twenty-six years, at the doctor's office. Both were shocked since we had not seen each other since 1989. They hugged and chatted and Miriam came out to see me in the parking lot. A healing has taken place. We speak on the phone. We've been to her house to eat, she to ours. Miriam, out of her own request, has become part of the family circle. We are reminded that healing can present itself in an un-expected way.

The young people of Jam Pak must be considered as part of my family circle. They are with me at least once ev-ery week, visiting, eating, making sure I take my pills and drink water, and watching out for me. They keep me prac-ticing and there is never a dull moment.

The new principal of Kinlichee Boarding School.

Everyone helps celebrate Tribal Leaders Day.

Ernest Ingraham, my friend and mentor, Dr. Annie Wauneka, famous Navajo educator, and me, Kinlichee Principal.

Flag ceremony.

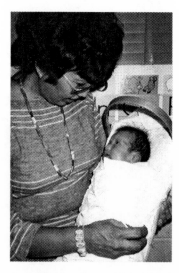

Lorraine Lewis, my right hand, and her new baby Chris.

Henry Shorty and his family from Cross Canyon – a home visit.

Sharing the milk at school.

*Jenny and Kris, new
sister and brother.*

Janette, Florine, Nyle, and Miriam – my
sisters-in-law and mother-in-law.

Sylvia and Ralph on their
way to Apache Lake.

My wide receiver.

286

Lal wins a trophy at a bodybuilding meet.

Many friends from Willie.

Sanjay, #86, open and ready.

Autographs after the game.

*Timothy, our three-toed western box turtle – we've
been feeding her for twenty years!*

*Sharing the grapes
with my hens.*

*St. Francis – we create
the copper sculpture
during Desert Storm 1992.
Let there be peace!*

Jam Pak in 1994 – I helped make the canjos.

Doug Scheeler – my flute student for eight years.

At Jenny's graduation from George Mason University, I meet Colonel Gabriel. He auditioned me for the United States Air Force Band in 1955. What a small world!

The Sparrow Band is born – January 1996.

My grandchildren's birthday present for me in 1998.

My sister Mavis raises two more boys in Jamaica
Fixing Twain's school tie.

291

Keeno says, "Me love you, Mama," to my sister Mavis.

Buddy helps me practice my cello.

Great Grandma Florine's last party – January 8, 2003.

We'll miss you always, Florine – February 15, 2003.

Our new friend, Howard Self, Executive Director of the American Family Coalition in Washington, D.C.

U.S. Representative Jeff Flake, of Arizona, presented the National Excellence in Parenting Award to us at the U.S. Capitol on July 23, 2003.

Gieselle Tambe-Ebot carries on the legacy of the harp; she was also my flute student and friend.

The bunkhouse on the Shandon, California ranch where we spent the summer of 2005 writing my story.

Favorite cattle – Victoria, Paintbrush, Eran, and Poncho Villa.

My brother-in-law shows me how to ride Cheyenne.

Jam Pak at the Tucson Bluegrass Festival – 2005.

Kris and his children
Ebony, Kris, Vance, Colton, Keasha, Haley.

Sanjay and family
Kristy, Kalpana, Tariq, Sanjay, Jalen, Makis.

With Liberty and Justice For All! I marched with
our friends and thousands of other people to find
the best solutions for undocumented workers. I
made it the whole three miles. April 10, 2006

All Will Be Well

Peanut brittle, cheese nips,
And blackberry tea –
Such a banquet for you and me.
Looking up to the Praying Hands –
Talking softly about our plans.
A moment away, a moment to spare
A moment to whisper a little prayer
That all will be well,
That all will be well.

Written by AC and me
August 18, 2004
while resting in the motor home at Gold Canyon Ghost
Town at the foot of the Superstition Mountains

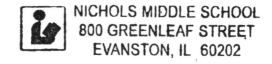

NICHOLS MIDDLE SCHOOL
800 GREENLEAF STREET
EVANSTON, IL 60202

About the Author
Vincent Collin Beach

Vincent Beach has seen a lot in the past 82 years – wars fought and peace enjoyed, bigotry endured and inclusion celebrated, loves found and loves lost, children born and children buried. Through it all, his mother's adages have helped sustain him. "Don't throw away your stick till you cross the river," she often told him. It was not till years later that he grasped the full meaning behind the saying.

Leaving behind his rural home in Jamaica, Vincent set out for a new life. He joined the British Royal Air Force in 1944 and served several years in England. Yearning to be a jazz musician, but without any background in music, he bought a pawnshop clarinet. In 1952, full of hope, he emigrated to the United States. He immediately encountered the ugliness of racism, retreated to England, but in 1955 returned to try once more to find the "American dream." He enlisted in the United States Air Force and enjoyed a 22-year career as a military bandsman. Two more careers, spanning 23 years, including 10 years as a counselor and school principal on the Navajo Reservation, and a community college instructor in political science and psychology in Chandler, Arizona, have provided Vincent with many opportunities to rely on the adages of his mother Miss Rosa.

He describes himself as an ordinary man from ordinary beginnings. Why then did he decide to write his autobiography? "I believe the stories of other people's lives are enlightening," he says. "Perhaps some thought or idea can be gleaned to make life's journey more satisfying."

He and his wife Anni, who helped him prepare his manuscript, received the "2003 National Excellence in Parenting Award" from the National Parents' Day Council at a ceremony in Washington, DC.

About the Co-Author
Anni Beach

Anni, Vincent's wife and partner, has served as a catalyst for bringing this book to publication. Although
much of the writing was done by Vincent over the course
of many years, Anni also taped and transcribed his stories,
and took personal dictation which gave her the opportunity
to question him in depth regarding events, emotions, and
philosophy. She helped Vincent research details to ensure
that the book is an accurate account of his life. And finally,
with Vincent by her side, she has woven the events of his
life and family into a remarkable story.

Born in 1943 to Ronald and Florine DuFresne of Vancouver, Washington, she was best known for her love of her
pets including a Nubian goat named Heidi and an assort-
ment of bantam chickens. Growing up in an environment
of social activism, she wanted to do something that would
help others. Finding just the right thing was difficult – health
education, agriculture, and social work were tested, but finally she became a teacher. Finding her way to the Navajo

Reservation in 1969, she served in the boarding school system for seventeen years.

Anni was as a substitute teacher in Chandler, Arizona schools for many years; a job she loved as she got to meet lots of people and play a lot of music on her mandolin. She continues to lead the Jam Pak Blues 'N' Grass Neighborhood Band, enjoy her family, pets, and most of all her husband Vincent whom she describes as "my hero and rock".

About the Publisher

Don't Throw Away Your Stick Till You Cross the River is published by Five Star Publications. One of Five Star's missions is to help authors create books that help foster tolerance and acceptance of the differences in others. President Linda F. Radke, who started the firm in 1985, has worked with hundreds of authors over the years; some famous, some obscure, but all with messages they wanted others to hear. She's garnered a long list of publishing awards along the way. Five Star is one of the country's leading small press publishers, offering consulting, book production, publishing, and full marketing services. Linda was recently named "Book Marketer of the Year" by Book Publicists of Southern California.

Printed in the United States
R2843400004B/R28434PG66546LVSX2BA/8}